P9-BZP-178
p. 46
p. 190
p. 86
p. 162
p. 104
p. 154
p. 26
p. 109
p. 77
p. 6

Nina
Garcia's
LOOK
BOOK

ALSO BY

NINA GARCIA

AND ILLUSTRATED BY

RUBEN TOLEDO

THE LITTLE BLACK BOOK OF STYLE

THE ONE HUNDRED

THE STYLE STRATEGY

ILLUSTRATIONS BY

RUBEN Toledo

voice
Hyperion ~ New York

Nina Garcia's

WHAT TO WEAR FOR EVERY OCCASION

LOOK BOOK

Copyright © 2010 Nina Garcia

All rights reserved. No part of this book may be used or reproduced in any manner whatsoever without the written permission of the Publisher. Printed in the United States of America. For information address Hyperion, 114 Fifth Avenue, New York, New York, 10011.

Library of Congress Cataloging-in-Publication Data

Garcia, Nina.
Nina Garcia's look book : what to wear for every occasion / Nina Garcia ; illustrations by Ruben Toledo.
p. cm.
ISBN 978-1-4013-4147-3
1. Clothing and dress. 2. Fashion. 3. Women's clothing. I. Title.
TT507.G353 2010
746.9'2—dc22 2010016511

Hyperion books are available for special promotions and premiums. For details contact the HarperCollins Special Markets Department in the New York office at 212-207-7528, fax 212-207-7222, or email spsales@harpercollins.com.

Book design by Shubhani Sarkar

FIRST EDITION

10 9 8 7 6 5 4 3 2 1

We try to produce the most beautiful books possible, and we are also extremely concerned about the impact of our manufacturing process on the forests of the world and the environment as a whole. Accordingly, we've made sure that all of the paper we use has been certified as coming from forests that are managed, to ensure the protection of the people and wildlife dependent upon them.

FOR WOMEN EVERYWHERE . . .

Contents

dating

night

holidays

life events

weddings

dream travel

CHIC TRANSIT AND STYLISH ADVENTURING

Nina
Garcia's
LOOK
BOOK

Introduction

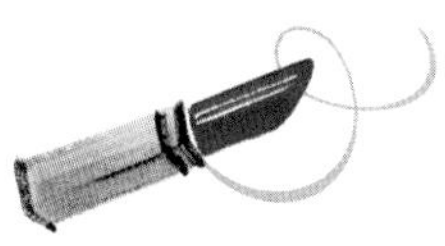

Know first who you are;
and then adorn yourself accordingly.

EPICTETUS

One of the most magical places on earth is a small island in the Caribbean called Mustique. With brilliant beaches, warm water, and lush vegetation, this tiny green swath of land is my idea of paradise. I go there to decompress from the frenetic pace of New York City and all the necessary and unnecessary pressures I place on myself at work and in life.

It was on Mustique that the genesis of this book took place, sparked by a conversation I overheard while lounging late one morning under an umbrella by the beach. I was reading a novel that wasn't nearly as interesting as the dialogue taking place between two women sitting near me. I couldn't see them and wouldn't have known they were there were it not for their animated discussion, their tempers on the brink of flaring the way they sometimes can when women are at odds. The older woman, whom I presumed to be the mother (I met her later at the hotel bar and confirmed this), was scolding her daughter about the merits of dressing appropriately now that she had graduated from college.

"You can't go around wearing sandals and jeans 24/7 anymore," the older woman almost barked. "Every occasion requires thought about how you look. You know this."

"But I didn't think I looked bad," her daughter whined.

"You can't tell me there aren't jobs out there after I ask what you wore to the interview and you tell me you put on those jeans!"

Oh dear, I thought. *Jeans to a job interview. She didn't.*

I instantly thought of my own mother, a beacon of elegance who would have threatened me with incarceration for that kind of transgression. In Colombia, where I was born and raised, women like my mother considered their appearance and personal grooming a matter of principle. There was never an occasion where she didn't show up looking picture-perfect.

Although I was supposed to be "on vacation" and far away from all things job related, I could not help thinking how this exact sort of conversation was probably taking place between mothers and daughters around the globe. From Delaware to Düsseldorf, I could almost hear the sea of mothers and daughters, each up in arms about the other's recurring faux pas. Frustrated moms eager to vanquish tattered T-shirts, torn jeans, dirty sneakers, and old flip-flops in a bonfire of oblivion. Desperate daughters insisting they will "literally die of embarrassment" if their mothers look too dowdy or, worse, continue raiding their daughters' closets for skintight jeans and microminis in misguided last-ditch attempts to regain the rebelliousness of their youth.

Then I thought about my girlfriends. I thought of the hundreds, if not thousands, of calls I field from them (and they from me) a couple of hours before we meet for an event, each and every call boiling down to the same question, repeated over and over: "What Should I Wear?!" Everyone has made that call, had that conversation, and wailed this question—what to wear to a rock concert, a first date, a funeral, or a Yankees game, a trade convention, or even to brunch with each other!

I don't do fashion, I am fashion.

COCO CHANEL

I firmly believe that 90 percent of the confusion that women feel when they are attempting to put together an occasion-specific ensemble is caused by *fear*: fear of breaking the "fashion rules," fear of violating some long-forgotten tradition, or the basic fear of looking bad. However, any undertaking based on fear is likely to fail—or, at the very least, it won't be much fun. And style is all about fun. Getting dressed for an occasion should not induce anxiety. It should be an exciting challenge to communicate who YOU are to the world, without saying a word. The most fabulous style icons are those women who know what the rules are and have the confidence to ignore them, push things to the edge, and yet flawlessly keep within the confines of what's appropriate.

Overbearing, too-stringent rules are the enemy of true style. But there *are* clues, contexts, and a fashion language that exists in any given situation. We've probably all heard the cliché "There is a right time and right place for everything." This is completely true for matters of style. Each moment calls for a different stylistic essence and a different sense of impact, and mastery of this balance is an art form—a very learnable art form. The key to style success is knowing what this essence is, and knowing how to effortlessly communicate in the language of fashion. You don't have to be fluent, but you want to be understood.

Take, for example, one of my least favorite fashion rules: the precept that no woman over the age of twenty-nine should wear a skirt shorter than two inches above the knee. Ridiculous! If you've got it, flaunt it, no matter your age. However, it's equally important to know in what context to flaunt it. If you meet someone for the first time and while she's talking to you, you're wondering why a person would wear a micromini skirt and knee-high boots to her son's soccer game, well, she might be a fascinating, quirky, intelligent woman; she may be up for a Nobel Prize; she may be a classically trained French pastry chef; or she could be the most loyal friend in the world (once you get to know her), but many people (including you) will never bother to try. They will dismiss her at hello. Making a good impression is about understanding boundaries, communication, social savvy, and my favorite factor: knowing thyself—and then translating the unstoppable force of YOU into the style language of every event and occasion you grace with your presence.

A great social success is a pretty girl who plays her cards as carefully as if she were plain.

F. SCOTT FITZGERALD

This book will lead you through the fashion lingo for some of life's basic occasions to ensure that your ensemble is always a flawless representation of you. You'll learn how to be appropriate without being prudish, creative without being too zany, and confident without being overbearing. Obviously, I could not include every single life event in this one volume. I pared the list to some of life's biggies; to the situations that cause most of our fashion stress. I've offered advice on the social graces of an occasion, factoids that have helped focus me and give me confidence throughout the years. The outfits I suggest for each situation are just that, *suggestions*. I've given you my ideal ensemble to illustrate each look, but I never want you to forget that really authentic style comes from within, and you must always remain stylistically true to yourself. Don't be afraid to add your own flair to my recommendations. Fearlessness is integral to innovation. Just remember that whatever you wear, wear it with sublime confidence.

Life is dynamic, ever changing, and fluid; so too must our sense of style move and evolve. Every one of us should constantly be honing our style skills and adjusting them to a changing audience. I'm always acutely aware of what I'm wearing and who will be seeing me in it. Believe me—there's pressure when you're deciding what to wear to a meeting with an iconic fashion designer or a member of the press. It can be terrifying. But instead of panicking, I stop, take a deep breath, and remember that I speak "fashion." And by the time you have read this book, you'll be able to speak the language of fashion too, at all the key moments of your life. True style is not about having a closet full of expensive and beautiful things, it is instead about knowing when, where, and how to utilize your collection. Whether you're more Lady Gaga or more Lady Bird Johnson, there is always "just the right thing" for you to wear, anywhere. Your job, with my help, is to figure out what that is.

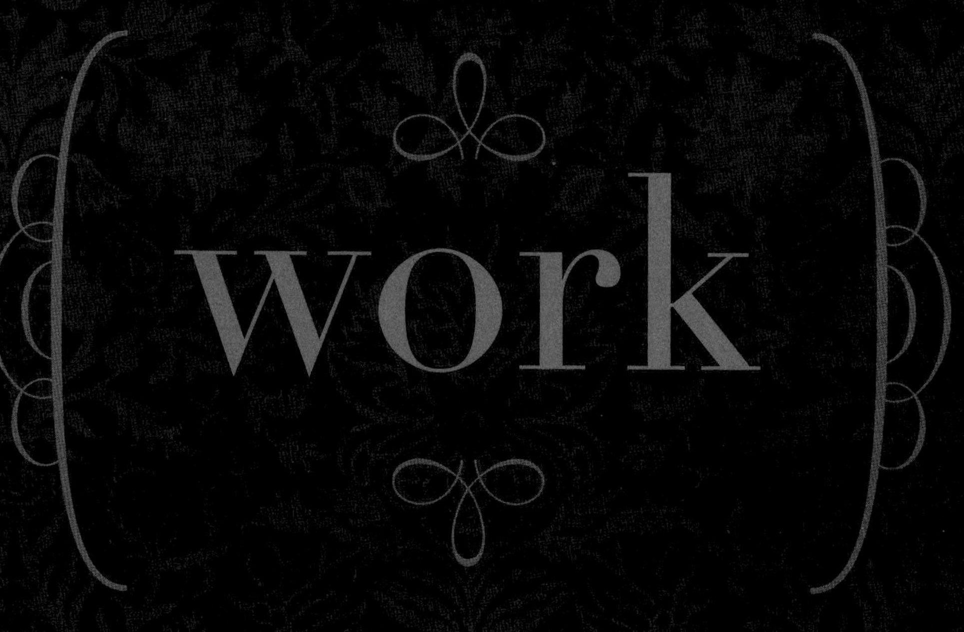

work

Power Chic

What to Wear to a Job Interview

There is no better way to start the *Look Book* than with the question we've all asked ourselves: What should I wear to a job interview? This, along with first dates, which we will, of course, explore later, is the mother of all first impressions, a minuscule slice of time when a potential employer gets a peek at your essence. Especially now, when competition is fierce and the stakes are higher, it is critical that you consider not only what you will say to impress your interviewer and sell yourself, but also how you will look the minute you walk into that office. Who will the employer see? How will that make her feel about you as a colleague? The smallest detail can set you apart from your competition. It's essential that you appear professional, capable, and confident without going overboard. Extremes of any kind are an absolute no-no. Your wardrobe should complement your skill set, never detract (or *dis*tract) from your assets. You want your ensemble to say, "I have good judgment, I am extremely competent, I am socially adept, and you are a true visionary if you choose to hire me."

It's a tall order to live up to, but I have faith in you.

> *You can have anything you want in life if you dress for it.*
>
> EDITH HEAD

Today's suit has so many options and variations that it never has to be stuffy or boring. In fact, a suit can be quite glamorous while still maintaining its business edge. I can't stress enough the importance of keeping your look relevant; fashion is cyclical and you've got to be aware of trends without becoming a slave to them. A suit says that you are serious, that you take the position seriously, and that you know how to make a great impression. A streamlined silhouette conveys structure and organization, two characteristics that your potential employers will surely seek in a candidate. A woman who walks into a room wearing a chic, modern take on the classic suit is immediately in the game.

So many women don't pay enough attention to the handbag they carry to a job interview. Details, girls! Your bag should go with your ensemble without being too matchy-matchy, and it should be very, very neat. Nothing makes a bad impression like having to search through a jumble of lipsticks, used tissues, breath mints, and God knows what else when you're looking for a pen. Be prepared and efficient. Do match the class of your bag to the level of the position you are seeking. If you are interviewing for a receptionist job, don't carry a Louis Vuitton Monogram. Never upstage the boss.

Even in the middle of summer, a jacket is a must to pull your outfit together. A jacket says poise and maturity, and it conveys the professional energy that you should radiate when you walk into that room. And, if you're anything like the rest of humanity, you perspire under pressure, so the more layers between your skin and the rest of the world, the better. A jacket may *feel* uncomfortable, but it looks cool, calm, and collected.

When striving to make a great business impression, you want everyone to focus on what you're saying without being distracted by what you're wearing. Avoid too many bright colors and bold patterns. Mind you, *judiciously* incorporating color or pattern into a slick outfit will get you noticed in the right way. If you opt for neutrals (navy, brown, gray, and the ubiquitous black), add a colorful belt or patterned tights. Or, wear a smart jacket with a bold pattern such as a hound's-tooth check or a frothy blouse in a vibrant hue, but keep the rest of your ensemble neutral.

A LIGHTER SHADE OF PALE

When in doubt, these chic hues are guaranteed to work together in perfect harmony.

Navy · Black
Brown · Navy
Loden · Gray
Gray · Aubergine
Camel · Ivory

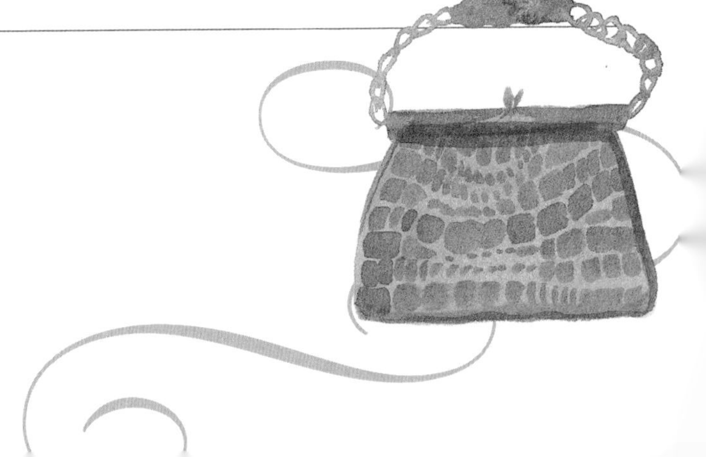

When I'm interviewing a prospective employee, I appreciate an eye-catching touch of flair. It's refreshing to see a woman who can artfully weave her individuality into an otherwise safe ensemble. But use your flair tactfully; always take a second and third look at yourself right before you walk out that door. I work in the fashion industry, where flair done right is always appropriate, but never forget your audience; be extremely sensitive to what sort of attire is appropriate for the job you are seeking.

JOB INTERVIEW STYLE *DON'TS*

- DON'T WEAR FUR. It can be controversial; not to mention it's a little over the top for a job interview.
- DON'T WEAR LOUD JEWELRY. The only kind of bling you should sport is something like a classic strand of pearls, a simple pendant on a delicate chain, or an equally minimal piece. Dazzle them with your wit and intelligence, not your baubles.
- DON'T WEAR HEAVY MAKEUP. Your look should be sweatproof and showcase your beautiful features.
- DON'T WEAR SHINY FABRICS. Unless perfectly executed, they come off as cheap and too informal.
- NO CLEAVAGE, NO GAPPING BETWEEN BUTTONS, NOTHING SEE-THROUGH. You're a girl that works. Not a working girl.
- NO WILD PATTERNS, AND KEEP RUFFLES AND EMBELLISHMENTS TO A MINIMUM. Too much pageantry at the first interview is too distracting. Simple and streamlined keeps the focus on you and your skills.

JOB INTERVIEW STYLE *DO'S*

You can only make one first impression, so make it your best. Be well groomed, pressed, and with not a hair out of place.

- DO WEAR A WATCH. A classic men's watch is not only functional but one of my favorite accessories for an all-business look. Your future boss will see that you've beautifully integrated punctuality into your style arsenal. And punctuality is a must.
- A MANICURE IS ESSENTIAL. Hands are so expressive; they cannot be overlooked. Keep your nail color chic and understated; avoid long acrylics and bright polish.
- DO SPIT OUT YOUR GUM. Fresh breath is a must, but no one looks good chewing on a wad of gum.
- DO YOUR HOMEWORK. Research the company and be prepared to think on your feet. Knowledge is power and Google is your friend here.
- EXPRESS YOUR PASSION FOR THE JOB AND RADIATE ORGANIZATION. Passion and organization are an unstoppable combination.

rules are made to be broken

Never wear black with brown or navy.

Rubbish. Black with brown, navy, or gray is a thoroughly modern twist on classic dressing.

> *It is your work in life that is the ultimate seduction.*
>
> PABLO PICASSO

It's unbelievably difficult to muster up sufficient enthusiasm to impress anyone when your current job situation makes you want to go home and watch hours of bad sitcoms or drink yourself into a comfortable stupor. So it's vital that you take care of yourself and keep a positive attitude during this process. Use the negative energy of your current situation as the starting point for your strategy to change it. And make sure to look fabulous doing it.

Other than what to wear, the job interview question I'm asked most often is, "What do you look for in an applicant?"

I look for someone who takes herself seriously without being overbearing or pushy. A woman who can think on her feet and come up with creative solutions, and someone who seems like she would be pleasant to work with in addition to being highly skilled. If a prospective employee seems uncomfortable or stiff in her clothes, she may be stiff and uncomfortable every day—not an appealing prospect. Your clothing is like a protective suit of armor—wear everything as if it were custom-made for you, as if you were born in it.

Practice your interview style with friends, get comfortable answering questions on a number of topics, and always research the company you are applying to. I love it when an interview feels like a conversation rather than an interrogation, and when the person I'm speaking with is really listening to what I say before she responds. Know your weaknesses but paint them in a positive light and don't be afraid to list your strengths. You are your own best advocate; too many women forget this. Also remember that you won't click with everyone; it's best to figure that out up front. You just may dodge a bullet if the position/employer combo is not the best fit for you. Success is just around the corner. Believe this, act on this, and it will be.

rule breakers we love

Queen Elizabeth I

Queen Elizabeth I personified the concept of dressing to impress. Her extravagant style influenced men and women throughout England and beyond, and intimidated her opponents. She lived by the philosophy that "more is more" and in so doing, created an empire. She's the ultimate can-do woman.

Start Strong

What to Wear on the First Day of Work

The details are not the details.
They make the design.

CHARLES EAMES

You did it. You landed the job. You have spent the night before this first day sleepless—excited and nervous about what this new position will bring, fantasizing about the possibilities for you and your future. The sky's the limit. But when the morning dawns, the outfits you thought about wearing don't seem right anymore, panic sets in, and that bright future you dreamed of is suddenly dark and stormy. The questions begin all over again: Should you wear the skirt or the pants? Are the heels you've planned on just too high? Is your statement piece making too much of a statement? I mean, unless you're attending the art opening of a Rhode Island School of Design student, is electric blue velour really ever appropriate for anything? Breathe. Get it together. You've got some quick planning to do.

The key word on your first day at a new job is DETAILS. You are the sum of all your details, the nuances that make you unique. Expect to be scrutinized by just about everyone during the first week or two. Nothing jolts energy into a work environment like the new girl. And how she is received will be shaped by the impression she makes at first glance.

THE coif THE face

A blow-dry is a must. Nothing compares to the polish and shine of properly blown out hair. It's the perfect finish to every outfit, so learn how to do it like a pro. Your hair shouldn't hide your face. Brush those sexy long bangs to the side.

Natural, neutral makeup is perfect for the office. No bright blue eye shadow and no glitter. Glow subtly, and leave the shimmer to after-hours and weekends. Finish your look off with rosy lipstick; it does wonders for your complexion in the harsh fluorescent lighting of most work environments.

Presumably you got a look at what the others generally wear when you first came in for your interview. For at least the first week amp the formality of your attire up a notch. But just a notch. It's essential to strike that delicate balance between relatability with your peers and respect from your superiors. You want to look approachable yet interesting, and most important, you want to make your boss proud.

PUT YOUR BEST FOOT FORWARD

How to become indispensable and upwardly mobile in the office—and in life:

- Anticipate problems and solve them resourcefully. Your initiative won't go unnoticed.
- Always say "Yes" to a challenge and give it your best effort.
- Never mix work and romance. I know it's tempting, but office romances are distracting and they rarely end well.
- Never make the same mistake twice.
- Ask questions; never stop learning about your position and your company.
- Always keep a notebook on hand to jot down notes. It'll pay off, believe me.

As always, I'm not telling you to completely suppress your own inimitable style (as if you could), but just to tailor it for the situation at hand. Let your flair emerge subtly on that first day. Your outfit should say, "Hello, I'm the best candidate for this job. I have the experience, the people skills, and the savvy to take this company to the next level." It doesn't matter whether you are an administrative assistant or a vice president, your ensemble should project skill and efficiency. People love to put a label on everything, especially in the office, so it's important that your initial label is one you can live with. It's not easy to undo a good first impression, but it's nearly impossible to reverse a bad one.

Use what you wore to the job interview that landed you the position as a guide, and plan your first day from there.

WHAT'S in YOUR bag?

Keep the bag simple and the contents neat. Do a weekly bag edit so you aren't always searching for your wallet in an endless abyss of receipts and business cards. Always bring your day planner, a pen or two, and mints. You never know what your boss might need at any given moment, so be prepared. Make sure the bag's size makes it easy to stow in a desk drawer.

WHAT YOU SHOULD WEAR

DRESS: Wear a frock that's professional but interesting. Look for unusual details like structured pleats or intricate seaming. A fabric with great texture, like cloque or bouclé, or a subtly unique pattern will intrigue and impress. Think Michael Kors with a hint of Christian Lacroix.

TROUSERS: Go for streamlined and modern trousers with clean lines.
SHIRT: There's something about a crisp, collared, white button-down shirt that makes us stand up a little straighter. A whimsical blouse with a little frill at the neck looks smashing under a structured jacket. The interplay between soft and crisp creates an unforgettable look.
JACKET: If you prefer to go the pants and jacket route, this is a great day to experiment with a different silhouette. You could wear a cropped, fitted jacket with strong, angular shoulders and high-waisted trousers or an oversize blazer with lean cigarette pants.
PUMPS OR BROGUES: Avoid stilettos or platforms unless you're absolutely sure they're appropriate for your office and that you can realistically spend an entire day wearing them. Go for something sleek and simple. Wedges are OK, but they can look casual or clunky with a suit, so choose wisely.
STOCKINGS: If you want to add a splash of color, this is the place to do it, but don't go too bright. You must look professional, and not like you're on leave from a stint with Cirque du Soleil.
ACCESSORIES: Simple, simple, simple. A small pendant or pearls. Wait until your second day to sport piles of lavalieres or a chunky statement piece. Don't wear anything that jingles or clanks.

---

rule breakers we love

Gloria Steinem

Ms. magazine cofounder Gloria Steinem showed women everywhere that *feminism* and *femininity* are not mutually exclusive concepts. She is smart, strong, and confident, and was sexy enough to famously go undercover for a story as a Playboy bunny in her quest to portray the state of women's rights. Her honey blond hair and oversized glasses became her trademark look. Create yours.

rules are made to be broken

It was unacceptable for women to wear pants on the floor in Congress until the nineties.

I can't believe it took that long for Congress to join the rest of the country. Women can wear pants anywhere they please. With impeccable tailoring, few pieces command as much respect.

Now that you have a good sense of what to wear on your first day of work, you should be able to sleep more soundly the night before. After all, wardrobe aside, sleep and rest are indispensable to keep your mind sharp and your creativity flowing for that first day.

Honoring Tuesday

What to Wear on the Average Workday

Nothing screams average day like a Tuesday. It's not Monday, with its weekend spillover and beginning-of-the-week stress. Nor does it have the relief of Wednesday, the beloved hump day, when time actually starts to work in our favor. It doesn't have the excitement of Thursday, which can mean an after-work night out with friends. And it is certainly not Friday, with its glorious taste of the weekend.

No, it's Tuesday: The Average Day.

This is actually the hardest day to pin down stylistically. Approach it as a personal exercise in style consistency. Dressing for the Average Day is about springboarding into who you want to become next. Now that you have shown your employers and colleagues who you are, start showing them who you want to be.

Appropriate wear for an average Tuesday at the office varies drastically from workplace to workplace. Context is everything and every industry has its own dress code—some tacit, others explicit. Of course, there's always a little leeway here and there, for you to express your individuality. Let your position, and the direction you want to go within the company, be important factors in deciding how you should dress for work. Always nail the average Tuesday. Always.

A bit of self-assessment is a great place to start.

- How do I want to be perceived by my coworkers, superiors, and clients?
- Will I be taken seriously in this outfit?
- Am I comfortable enough to roll up my sleeves and get to work?
- Am I TOO comfortable?
- Will I stand out from my coworkers? In a bad way?

> *The basic elements of any businesswoman's wardrobe should rely on this trio: simple casual suits, tailored dresses, and good separates.*
>
> EDITH HEAD

Be sure to answer these questions carefully.

If you're an assistant, whether you like it or not, how you look reflects on your boss as well. You want to show your employer that you are a team player and that you honor your position and the company in general. The way you look matters for people other than yourself.

Whether you wear corporate, business casual, or plain casual attire to work, the key is to keep your look pulled together and polished: Be neat, relevant, and modern. Edit yourself and acknowledge the tone of the office. The best piece of advice given to me when I was starting out was to find a "style mentor." You know, the woman at work who already has the job you dream of getting one day; she always looks amazingly put together with that perfect blend of classic and modern, professional yet relaxed, *and* she knows the business inside and out. Study her; emulate her.

rule breakers we love

Christiane Amanpour

Christiane Amanpour, anchor for ABC News's *This Week* and former chief international correspondent for CNN, is a brilliant journalist and a profoundly beautiful woman. She looks equally splendid reporting from the comfort of a posh studio or from a harrowing, and most definitely unglamorous, war zone. Ms. Amanpour doesn't really have an "average" workday. But her look is always practical, streamlined, and spot-on.

WHAT YOU SHOULD WEAR

Everyone needs a dash of flair here and a splash of color there. Here are a few ways to give your professional look a modern edge:

- Break up your suit by pairing the jacket with a black knee-length skirt.
- Give your classic black pumps a lift with textured tights.
- Break out of the blazer rut and try a jacket with a different silhouette—strong shoulders, architectural or geometric tailoring, maybe even a peplum if you're feeling flirty. Perhaps a fabulous cropped jacket. Or a traditional blazer in a nontraditional fabric like sateen or a colorful check.
- Wear distinctive yet chic jewelry like a wood ring or a cuff.
- Do the white shirt with a twist like a ruffle, strong shoulders, or an origami detail.

BORROW FROM THE BOYS

A woman wearing something from a man's closet expresses supreme confidence in her own femininity.

- ORDER AN ASSORTMENT OF CUSTOM-MADE SHIRTS. A great cotton shirt that's monogrammed and tailored to fit you perfectly is the height of sophisticated elegance.
- WEAR A MEN'S OVERSIZE COAT. Roll up the sleeves and belt it for casual chic. Keep it loose and open for a more relaxed vibe.
- CUFFLINKS ARE A FABULOUS AND UNUSUAL ACCESSORY. A perfect way to stand out from the office drones.
- A SIGNET RING IS A SIMPLE, CLASSIC ADORNMENT. When you want some sparkle but nothing froufrou, go signet.
- A MEN'S WATCH IS ONE OF MY FAVORITE BUSINESS ACCESSORIES. It's classic, practical, and demonstrates you have great style and great timing.
- PIN-STRIPED OR CHALK-STRIPED MEN'S TROUSERS make you look a little taller and stand a little straighter.
- TWEEDS ARE SMART AND WORK WONDERFULLY AS SEPARATES. And they never wrinkle, so they're perfect for travel.

The greater the limitations, the more innovative you are forced to be. Think of it as a challenge. Put together an avant-garde look using just a gray three-piece suit, two accessories, stockings, and shoes. On a Tuesday!

I know that sometimes it seems impossible to make the Average Day shine. But once you're looking good, you'll start feeling good, and you'll be able to come up with even more amazing, groundbreaking ideas at work.

On the subject of dress almost no one,
for one or another reason,
is indifferent; if their own clothes do not
concern them, somebody else's do.

ELIZABETH BOWEN

Gal Friday

What to Wear on Casual Friday

If men can run the world,
why can't they stop wearing neckties?
How intelligent is it to start the day
by tying a little noose around your neck?

LINDA ELLERBEE

Ah, Casual Friday. That longed-for day; the finish line is visible, the beginning of weekend liberty. TGIF. Say it twice. TGIF. This is the day you can chat a bit longer with your office mate, laugh a little louder, extend your coffee break by a few minutes, and when the boss may actually leave early to get a head start on the weekend. Friday is the king of days, as far as the workweek is concerned. *Casual* Friday, however, is another story entirely.

What is really meant by Casual Friday? Is it plain casual, business casual, weekend casual, or slacker casual? The idea of Casual Friday has caused quite a bit of debate. You shouldn't wear pajamas or sweats to work, ever. You probably shouldn't wear a leather mini either. So just how casual is it?

Quite frankly, and I know I'm in the minority here, I prefer not to take advantage of Casual Friday at all—perhaps it's because I'm in the fashion industry, where one's attire is judged a bit more harshly. Casual Friday seems to me like a fashion disaster waiting to happen, with the possibility of some poor colleague prancing into the office in a poufy romper or, worse, overalls. I think the whole concept complicates dressing for work. People tend to abuse this collective social laxness and end up revealing a part of themselves that should really be left at home.

Casual Friday was created so that men could forgo wearing a suit and tie one day a week. Since it is almost universally acceptable for women to interchange trousers with skirts in a business setting, for women there really isn't too much of a point to this idea. We may be relieved not to have to endure heels and a suit jacket, but overall, the most important wardrobe consideration women have on Friday is how to transition from the office to happy hour and the weekend.

Try to equate your weekend wardrobe with your weekend life. Office is office and leisure is leisure—it's that simple. When your boss asks how your weekend was, you don't say, "Well, I was so stressed out from the office that I went out Friday night, drank too much, and broke the heel on one of my favorite blue stilettos too." No, you answer, "I spent Saturday catching up on chores around the house and I went to the park on Sunday. Wasn't the weather great?" Likewise, your ensemble should be appropriately edited for the office.

It only takes a bit of planning and a little creativity to transform everyday office attire into something chic and cocktail-worthy. The key here is layering. Peel away your day look to reveal a glamorous, glitzy outfit, and you'll be ready to start your weekend in under fifteen minutes.

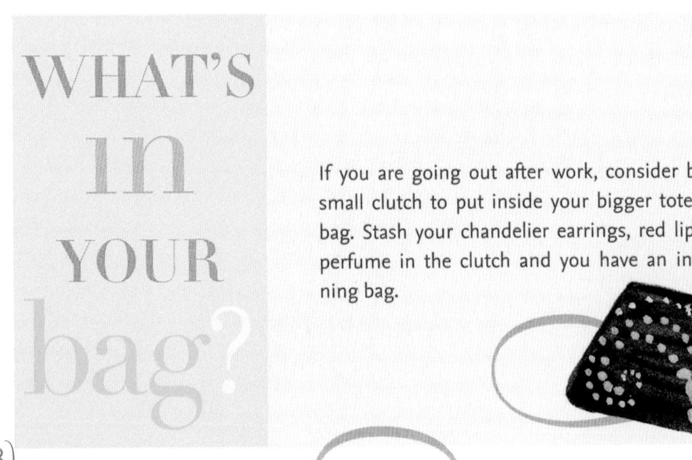

If you are going out after work, consider bringing a small clutch to put inside your bigger tote or handbag. Stash your chandelier earrings, red lipstick, and perfume in the clutch and you have an instant evening bag.

WHAT YOU SHOULD WEAR

- Trade your slouchy trousers for a sexy pencil skirt.
- Belt your jacket to accentuate your waist, or take it off and just go with the tank or shirt you so wisely have on underneath.
- Dab on an evening fragrance.
- Add a few accessories like earrings, a statement necklace, or a cuff.
- Refresh your makeup with a little more eyeliner and a second coat of mascara, and let your hair down.
- Change into a pair of outrageous heels. Outrageous shoes impart instant glam.
- Throw on a faux fur wrap or a scarf and it's a whole new fabulous you.

THE MYSTERY OF CASUAL FRIDAY

There are a few theories about who invented Casual Friday. Some say it originated in the fifties as a way to boost morale at the office. Others (including Levi Strauss) believe it was created in the seventies by Levi Strauss, as a way to boost sales of khakis. Still others credit the nineties dot-com boom for popularizing less formal office attire.

In 2005 the Japanese government instituted a casual dress code to reduce energy use in the summer (cooler clothes, less air-conditioning). This move was extremely unpopular with the Japanese, who are accustomed to wearing a suit and tie every day.

Showtime Chic

What to Wear to an Important Meeting or Presentation

For many of us, a whole career may be defined by how well we execute our first important presentation. Speaking to a room full of people is one of those tests the universe throws at you to see how well you can catch. When you're asked to prepare and present information, along with your analysis and recommendations, the result may be the difference between getting that desired promotion, or not; gaining the respect of your coworkers, or not; getting to the next level of success, or not. And don't forget: A successful presentation is an immeasurable boost to your self-esteem.

> *Your business clothes are naturally attracted to staining liquids. This attraction is strongest just before an important meeting.*
>
> SCOTT ADAMS

Whenever an important presentation or meeting looms, it's time to bring out the power suit. Ladies, again, this does not have to be a "suit" in the traditional sense. What I mean by "power suit" is an outfit that perfectly captures the energy of your professional efforts. You want your impeccably constructed outfit to project confidence and proficiency while you blow everyone's minds with your creativity and intellect. THAT's a power suit.

> *Take your work seriously, but never yourself.*
>
> MARGOT FONTEYN

Women have come so far in the past few decades. We no longer need to hide our femininity, or look "mannish," in order to project a powerful image. You can and should embrace your femininity while rocking that power suit. Don't be afraid of slightly overdressing. Going that extra fashion mile lets everyone know that you take your job seriously and that you respect their opinions. In turn, they will respect you.

I cannot stress enough the importance of quality and construction when dressing for a presentation. There's something divine about a woman in a body-conscious blazer and skirt that flawlessly show off her curves without appearing too suggestive. These structured suits and well-tailored numbers are like harnesses of strength, ensuring you look sharp and sophisticated.

rule breakers we love

Eva Perón

Eva Perón, second wife and political partner of President Juan Perón, spoke to all of Argentina. Her suits fit perfectly and epitomized the gorgeous structure that garments from the forties and fifties possessed. With her signature scarlet lips, and not a hair out of place, her style is legendary and her charisma is unparalleled.

When giving a presentation you must exude confidence, even when you're incredibly nervous. Posture is key and your wardrobe is your armor. Shoulders back, ladies. Spanx, a good bra, and anything else that you have in your body-shaping arsenal won't hurt either. In addition to a strong silhouette, color is of the utmost importance. Think carefully about the message you want to convey and choose your palette accordingly. Are you projecting sober austerity? Steel gray will work. Brisk efficiency? Think black and white, or charcoal pinstripes. Kindly, instructive authority? Choose peach, camel, or tweed.

> *Clothes can suggest, persuade, connote, insinuate, indeed lie, and apply subtle pressure while their wearer is speaking frankly and straightforwardly of other matters.*
>
> ANNE HOLLANDER

How should you prep for your presentation? Create a look that communicates assurance and friendliness while also showing you off at your fabulous best. Think it through. Envision yourself moving through your tasks at work with aplomb, and shining like a star when it is actually showtime. You can do it.

Material Girl

What to Wear When Asking for a Raise

> *I buy expensive suits. They just look cheap on me.*
>
> WARREN BUFFETT

Requesting a raise from your boss is one of the most daunting experiences you will ever have to endure. Women, especially, are often hesitant to demand the fiscal remuneration they deserve, hoping that the boss will spontaneously reward their hard work. Unfortunately this doesn't happen as often as it should, so you've got to take the initiative and be prepared to make your case when the time is right. With the perfect look, you'll command respect, bolster your case, and project your worth.

It's the buildup to asking that does the most damage to one's psyche. Most people have to take several days (or weeks) to work up the nerve to approach their boss about a raise, and most require copious self-affirmations and numerous pep talks from friends and family before they are able to gather the courage to march into the boss's office and lobby for what is often a well-deserved pay hike. You have to look unstoppable and, even more important, you have to *feel* unstoppable.

In one visual punch, your outfit has to say: "I'm invaluable to this company and to you. I know what it takes to get the job done, as I have proven time after time. My intrinsic value to this company should be reflected in my salary. I won't take no for an answer." But the outfit must simultaneously communicate: "AND I love working here and I'm absolutely loyal to you. If you give me this raise, I'll do an even better job than the great job I already do! I promise."

This is a very tall order for one outfit.

> *I only want people around me who can do the impossible.*
>
> ELIZABETH ARDEN

Approach the occasion formally, just not *too* formally—you don't want to appear to be trying too hard (thus conveying the possibility that you're anticipating a "no"). Wearing a serious, all-business outfit may provide the perfect shield for you to do what you need to do to and, as they say, "bring home the bacon."

rule breakers we love

Rachel Maddow

Every night on television, we see Rachel Maddow wearing her traditionally "male" suit. With her minimal on-air look, she has smashingly turned femininity on its head by showing how an assertive, intelligent woman—wearing bare makeup, a dark suit jacket, and a boyish haircut—can be not only compelling, but sexy too.

WHAT YOU SHOULD WEAR

Obviously, you must adjust for your own sense of style. But if I had a friend call me the night before she was going to ask for a raise or promotion, I'd recommend:

SUIT: Great tailoring and a perfect fit are essential for creating a sense that no team is a team without your presence. A perfect fit means your suit should skim your body—not cling to it or envelop it. If a skirt is part of the suit, make sure the darts are flat, the pleats sharp, and the length in perfect proportion to the rest of your ensemble; if you opt for trousers, there should be no pulling at the crotch, a formed waistband, and they should hang beautifully. Always remember that this doesn't have to be a traditional suit; you just need strong, coordinated pieces.

SHIRT: Your blouse should be as crisp and tailored as your suit. A too high or tight collar can make you look a bit rigid, so keep the shirt loose but never unbutton anything lower than the third button from the top. A pretty, romantic blouse complements a highly structured look beautifully. Soften the hard edges of a suit with ruffles or a warm rosy color.

SHOES: Wear strong, assertive shoes that force you to stand a bit straighter and taller when you stride confidently into your boss's office. Try pumps with solid high heels. Not chunky, mind you; perhaps something round and tapered.

COLOR: Gray connotes strength. Black is also a great "I mean business" color, but don't fall into the trap of wearing black just to be safe; it might not be safe for you. As Coco Chanel said, "The best color in the whole world is the color that looks good on you."

Other last-minute touches to keep in mind: Bring a lint roller and a stain stick to work to ensure that the look you worked so hard to achieve is not marred by a random piece of lint or spilled coffee. Also, run to the ladies' room for a quick mouthwash, because there is nothing like clean, fresh breath to make you feel awake and alert.

BEYOND THE SUIT: A PRACTICAL CHECKLIST

- List your accomplishments over the past year and highlight those that build your case.
- Be ready to show why you not only fulfill the needs of your job, but help support the company's larger business ideology.
- Be assertive, but not pushy.
- If an actual raise in salary is not an option, be prepared with a Plan B, a few other ways the company can acknowledge your work (perhaps a new job title, larger expense account, more vacation, etc.).
- Timing is crucial. Most experts agree that the end of the workday is the best possible time of day to ask for a raise.

Finally, make sure your entire ensemble fits together seamlessly and looks as though it was made for you. Your silhouette should be sleek and modern. You're a blade. Channel your inner gladiator. Before you make the pitch, take a few minutes to collect your thoughts, do some deep breathing, stand up straight, steel your shoulders, and know that you deserve this. You're ready to fight for this—and win.

Work and Play

What to Wear to an Office Party

Office parties can be the stuff of legend. Every workplace has stories about what happened to so-and-so at last year's Christmas party, gasp. And horrid tales of things gone awry at conference cocktail parties and trade show dinners when lines are blurred, liquor imbibed, and rumors ignited. Let's face it, all of this is fun if no one gets hurt. But it's even more fun if you had *nothing* to do with the ensuing drama. Discussions of disastrous office party incidents are a time you don't want your name mentioned. Trust me.

With that in mind, planning an ensemble for an office party is part of keeping yourself out of the gossip fray, and it requires a delicate balance. Every day I receive emails from women who want to know what's appropriate for office festivities. It is a party, right? Yes, but it is also work, and what you wear will affect how you are perceived at the office for days, weeks, months, and maybe even years to follow. You want to look festive, but not tarty; you want to look professional, but not stuffy. Your outfit should say, "No sweat, I can hang and have fun like anyone else, but I'm also that person you can count on. Even here."

This may seem a lot to ask from an outfit, but this look is really quite simple to achieve.

> *The truly fashionable are beyond fashion.*
>
> CECIL BEATON

Style is not neutral;
it gives moral directions.

MARTIN AMIS

Your task will be slightly easier if everyone is going straight to the party from work, because no one will expect you to dress up much beyond regular office attire. Most office parties that are more formal will specify a dress code on the invitation. Follow it. If the invitation says black tie, you have to ratchet the style-meter to its highest; if the invitation says cocktail or festive attire, keep the style-meter high, but not at nosebleed elevation.

The office party is almost always an annual event, and it typically occurs around the holidays. Propriety is of the utmost importance. In many cases higher-ranking executives will be in attendance and you do not want them to notice your outfit before they notice you, unless, of course, fashion *is* your job. For everyone else: Don't let your ensemble upstage your professional persona. Don't let all of the time and effort you put into your work be undone by the wrong party look.

My go-to ensemble for any office party is a chic, flowy, luxurious pant with a tuxedo-style jacket and a nice silk shirt, or a tailored and narrow tuxedo-style trouser, topped with a gorgeous silk shirt, and finished with a glamorously understated jacket.

Keep the sparkle to a minimum; this is not the place to go wild with the sequins, paillettes, spangles, and so forth. This is also not the place for ultra laid-back boho chic. Leave your inner gypsy at home. Wear one striking statement piece, like a necklace or chandelier earrings. Office parties are for small talk and networking, not for unnecessary opulence and overly long explanations of where you got your jewelry.

Last but definitely not least, don't overindulge in the cocktails or the food. Restraint is a virtue at the office party.

Company Party Dress Code: Formal

DRESS: Think simple, classic, chic. Floor-length (only if it's black tie) or just below the knee is best. And definitely nothing above the knee; that's for your weekend life. Black always works but it can be severe; a rich brown or deep aubergine are excellent alternatives, and don't be afraid to go for another color when you know it looks stunning on you.

SHOES: Sleek, sophisticated pumps or silk ballet flats. If you do want to make a statement, stunning shoes are an excellent way to add a touch of zest to low-key glamour. Just remember, no stripper shoes; a decadent pair of Louboutins will do.

Company Party Dress Code: Cocktail or Festive Attire

DRESS: Opt for a simple, elegant sheath, highlighted by one beautiful accessory like a vintage brooch or a simple sculptural pendant. A strong solid color is the perfect backdrop for a dramatic piece of jewelry. A tasteful sprinkling of sequins or beading will keep your look interesting. Always bring a scarf or a light cardigan, just in case you feel the need to cover up a bit more.

SHOES: Just like the dress, keep them fairly simple. Not too, too high; make sure that you can walk in them. You'll need to make a fast escape when everything is wrapped up so you can meet your date at another destination and have some real fun.

DON'TS FOR THE COMPANY OFFICE PARTY

- NO PLUNGING NECKLINES or other distractions—eyes up.
- NO MICROMINIS. Again, eyes up.
- KEEP RUFFLES TO A MINIMUM. You aren't frivolous; you're a powerful career woman.
- NO LUCITE HEELS. I'm sure I don't have to explain why.

Your hair should be up but not too high. Aim for smooth elegance, and a clean, rather than beehive upsweep. An updo is perfect because it sits in place neatly all day.

Makeup-wise, an office party is not the ideal venue for the smoky eye. Save that for your cabaret night. I like a very clean, minimal approach to the face for these types of functions. Mascara and a neutral shadow on the eyes, rosy cheeks, and scarlet lips are everything you need. Stash a little bottle of your favorite perfume in your bag, but nothing too overbearing.

> *What I don't like about office Christmas parties is looking for a job the next day.*
>
> PHYLLIS DILLER

The Sweatpants Trap

What to Wear When You Work from Home

The twenty-first century is brimming with change. Witness the incredible technology that allows us to redefine our occupations and our workplace. I have friends who have ridden into the corporate sunset and transitioned into life as full-time freelancers, and other friends who have launched businesses from the comfort of their own homes. Although I'm sometimes envious of these lifestyles, working from home does pose some serious style dilemmas.

Initially, of course, being able to wear pajamas all day if you feel like it is part of the lure of working from home—that and setting your own schedule. So why have I dedicated an entire chapter to what one wears while working from home? Because if you have a job that doesn't require you to check in at an office or take the occasional meeting, you can be on a very slippery slope from being home and comfortable to looking like a disheveled mess who panics every time the doorbell rings and you realize someone may actually see you in this state. Style *is* like a muscle. If you don't exercise it, you lose it. The more you schlep around in your drawstring pants and boyfriend tees, the less you're going to be able to pull your look together when necessary. Likewise, the more you walk out of the house feeling like a cool million bucks, the more you are going to want to get out and see people who can help you with your business. So, entrepreneurs, home workers, and freelancers of the world, let's work those style muscles.

Structure is as essential in life as it is in a beautifully tailored garment. When you don't have to be out of the house by a certain hour every day, it's a really good idea to set some kind of schedule and force yourself to adhere to it. This includes (and at best begins with) dressing in the morning as if you're actually going elsewhere to work. Getting dressed and

ready to begin the day at a specific time enables you to be more productive. Do not kid yourself: It's easy to lose focus at home; you're surrounded by chores that need doing, books you mean to read, the television, and no one checking over your shoulder to see how often you're on Facebook. *Looking* as though you are going to work puts you in the right frame of mind for getting the job done. And, if the dog won't stop dropping her ball at your feet in that adorably obnoxious way, or your bartender neighbor is playing loud music all day—you can just pack everything up, head to a quiet café, and soldier on, looking great and put together.

> *The woman who can create her own job is a woman who will win fame and fortune.*
>
> AMELIA EARHART

Obviously, business corporate attire isn't necessary at home unless that's truly your core style. Instead, take the freedom your work environment affords you, and experiment with new looks each day. By styling yourself in different ways, you will have fun and feel energized, plus you will be "practicing" looks for other occasions when you do need to leave the house. Dressing for home allows you to wear clothes that look great, but that you would never wear in a traditional office. And don't forget the shoes! You can take them off right away (you are at home, after all), but it's never a complete ensemble without the perfect shoe. Practice your style . . . since you can.

I've created some of my best outfits by remixing or re-accessorizing my separates on a whim. Many times what doesn't look splendid at first will grow on you over the course of a day. Or you'll add or remove a layer without even thinking about it and voilà! It's so freeing when you're not dressing to impress anyone but yourself. If you are lucky enough to work from home, you are lucky enough to run your own schedule. So carve out some time each day to play dress-up, and fine-tune your sense of style.

MAKE IT WORK (FROM HOME): IT'S ALL IN THE ATTITUDE

- SCHEDULE A MID-AFTERNOON WALK. Fresh air is a must for fresh ideas.
- TAKE A LUNCH BREAK. Don't fall into the all-day-snack-a-thon trap.
- SET UP A QUIET, ORGANIZED WORK AREA. It will do wonders for your productivity.
- START THE MORNING WITH A JOG OR SOME YOGA. Get the juices flowing.
- LIMIT YOUR WORKDAY TO EIGHT HOURS. This will force you to be efficient and focused.
- MAKE IT A POINT TO HAVE FRESH FLOWERS IN YOUR WORK AREA. Dress your workroom as well as yourself.

While experimenting with your personal style, play with your hair and makeup too. Try a new do. Set your hair in rollers or blow it out straight. Consider whatever you normally do, then flex the opposite muscle. Do the same with your accessories. Remember that change breeds creativity and vice versa. You are the captain of your ship, the envy of office drones everywhere. Take advantage of the freedom you have. Your fresh, new look may ignite that rejuvenating spark that comes with knowing you are the master of your destiny.

If I want to knock a story off the front page, I just change my hairstyle.

HILLARY RODHAM CLINTON

Come Fly with Me

What to Wear on a Business Trip

The nature of my job takes me all over the world. The downside is that I'm away from my family for weeks on end; the upside is that I'm not only blessed with the opportunity to see the world, but I visit different countries and cities so often I have friends to call for drinks everywhere I go. My spring and fall trips for fashion week in London, Milan, and Paris are by far my busiest times away from home, but they are also my favorite. And although I'm more than a pro at knowing just what to take with me, there is still that small seed of doubt when I check my luggage at the airport. My heart begins to race. Have I forgotten something? Probably. The key to minimizing this anxiety is to prepare, prepare, prepare.

Packing for a business trip can be a nightmare—you can't count on being able to buy something you've forgotten once you land. I mean, how are you supposed to know where to go for a pair of Spanx in Tokyo? Even if you knew where to shop, your busy schedule may not leave time for a trip to the nearest boutique. So, ladies, planning and strategy are required to fit the necessary array of career-defining looks into one bag.

Before you even pull out your suitcase, and especially if you've never before been to your destination, do some research. Knowledge is power; you will be the envy of all your less prepared colleagues if you know the vital local information.

The Vital Business Travel Questions

- What is the climate/weather forecast for the time you're there?
- Is this a big city, small town, suburb?
- Is there cultural fashion etiquette that I should be aware of?
- What business sector will I be interacting with and what is that sector's business style?
- What sort of meetings will I be attending? Board meetings, presentations, seminars, parties?
- What business-centric social events will I be attending?

If you're daunted by these questions, don't panic. Business attire is fairly universal, and thanks to globalization, we're all more familiar with each other's customs than in previous eras. Answer these questions, focus on packing the basics, and embrace the concept of layering, which will help to keep you comfortable, efficient, and dashing.

BUSINESS TRAVEL *DO'S*

- CHOOSE FABRICS THAT DON'T WRINKLE EASILY, such as wool, rayon, and cotton blends.
- INVEST IN YOUR BUSINESS STYLE ESSENTIALS, including proper blouses, skirts, and trousers; they're well worth the money.
- BRING LAYERS. Pile them on or pare them down as needed.
- ERR ON THE SIDE OF FORMALITY WHEN TRAVELING, but never to the point of being miserably uncomfortable.
- PACK AT LEAST ONE DAY BEFORE YOU LEAVE. That way, when you wake up in the middle of the night in a cold sweat because you forgot that extra pair of stockings, there's still time to throw them in. Avert the crisis before it even happens.

Day Gear

Presumably you will need to wear a suit or businesslike ensemble on more than one day of the trip, so pack looks that are easy to mix and match. Choose one or two foundation pieces, like a simple black or navy dress, and build all your outfits upon those. You never know when a meeting will run long, leaving you only ten minutes to get ready for dinner, so plan to go from day to evening with minimal adjustments. Keep it simple. Think chic, tailored, and practical. You can always throw in fun accessories like patent leather belts, cocktail rings, or bib necklaces to change up the look of each outfit, and still rely on your foundation pieces as your perfect base. You'll be amazed at the difference a nuanced touch of accessorizing can make. You can pack light and still look fresh for each occasion on the trip.

Evening Gear

Unless there's a very formal dinner or party, your foundation pieces can transform into festive evening attire in a snap. Loosen up your hair, shed the blazer, add a little glimmer here and there with a stronger lipstick and eye color, slip on your heels, and spritz an invigorating mist of evening perfume. You'll be stunning and cocktail-ready in under thirty minutes.

rule breakers we love

Benazir Bhutto

The late former prime minister of Pakistan was a beautiful woman and a leader whose wardrobe was always a perfect expression of herself and was always suitable in a complex array of international and national settings. Ms. Bhutto effortlessly blended traditional looks like a head scarf and kohl eyeliner with contemporary business suits. She commanded respect and remained true to her cultural roots—no small task for a woman in the male-dominated profession of business and politics.

Simple Travel Checklist

DRESS: Two lightweight, tailored, A-line or narrow sheaths that can be worn with a jacket for day and brightened up with a few key accessories for evening. At least one must be an LBD (little black dress); these are your base garments. Go for high-quality, impeccable pieces in fabrics that feel great against your skin.

TROUSERS/SKIRT: Pack a pair of smart black trousers, or a lean pencil skirt, that go well with your jacket. Remember the importance of proportion and silhouette when planning your ensembles. You always want to cut a dashing figure.

BLOUSE: Bring at least three tops. A white button-down shirt is a must. If you want a touch of color, choose a pastel or neutral—something that will match everything else you've packed. Monogrammed shirts add a chic touch. And rich fabrics, such as silk or satin, go from day to night like a dream.

VEST/CARDIGAN: When you want a more casual look, leave the jacket behind and throw on a vest or cardigan. A vest is an easy way to bring some interest to your ensemble and it's a sharp look. A dainty cashmere cardigan is always ladylike, and a heavier, belted cardigan is a softer take on the jacket.

JACKET: Tailored, tailored, tailored. I can't stress this enough. Make sure it goes with everything else you've packed. A warm gray, black, or navy blazer can be instantly transformed simply by changing what you have on underneath or adding a scarf or belt.

COAT: A trench is always appropriate for business. It's chic, versatile, and timeless. It may just be the perfect coat.

SHOES: Always pack at least two pairs of shoes, one for day and one for evening. Choose your most comfortable and versatile pair of heels. Don't go for the pony hair bootie on this type of trip. If you prefer, wear business flats. Patent leather is gorgeously weatherproof. Remember this basic rule when packing shoes: You don't want to be thinking about your feet the whole time you're away, so pack something you can walk in. Nothing brand new; that's just begging for blisters.

ACCESSORIES: Remember what we said about the details? You will rely on these vital tidbits to create the illusion that you've packed an entire wardrobe. Bring a scarf for a dash of color and warmth. A belt is key; you can wear it with the dresses, jacket, and cardigan to create different looks. Bring a few well-chosen pieces of jewelry, and always, always a watch. Think of your accoutrements as subtle visual commentary about who you are. Do you have an affinity for vintage objects, or are you a minimalist to the core?

QUICK GUIDE: STYLE IN THE GLOBAL WORKPLACE

- INDIA: Pantsuits are much more acceptable for women than skirts. A pant is a primary component of traditional women's *salwar* suits. Vibrant colors of any sort reign supreme.
- CHINA: Very conservative. Dark suits, skirts with a hem below the knee, and low- or no-heeled shoes are the rule.
- RUSSIA: Wool suits, fur, and darker conservative colors prepare Russian women for their icy climate.
- FRANCE: Scarves at all times, tied in every possible way. Tailoring is perfection, always stylish, and sexy, sexy, sexy. Appropriately sexy, that is.
- GERMANY: Neat and flawlessly groomed. Long fingernails are frowned upon. And absolutely no open-toed shoes.
- ITALY: Simple elegance and shoes, shoes, shoes.
- SPAIN: Funky and avant-garde. Colors, patterns, and textures are celebrated in every way.
- MEXICO: High heels and high style. Anything goes as long as it celebrates femininity.
- SWEDEN: Laid back. Androgynous. Skirts and dresses are never required.

Being powerful is like being a lady.
If you have to tell people you are, you aren't.

MARGARET THATCHER

CARRY-ON 101

- Pack makeup and sundries in a midsize clutch that can be worn for evening but doubles as a traveler's survival kit.
- Ballerina slippers that fold into a small pouch just in case you can't keep those heels on for one more second.
- A fountain pen. I love a beautiful, cherished pen; it speaks volumes about the owner.
- A cardholder. Contacts are gold and a cardholder is organized perfection.
- Personalized stationery makes a lasting impression when you need to pass a note.
- A sewing kit for those little emergencies.
- Make your carry-on a good-quality, minimal, and logo-free pull suitcase.

Now embark on your business travels with confidence, ready to take on the world. *And don't forget your cell phone charger*—that's an even bigger disaster than packing the wrong shoes.

dating

Coquette 101

What to Wear on a First Date

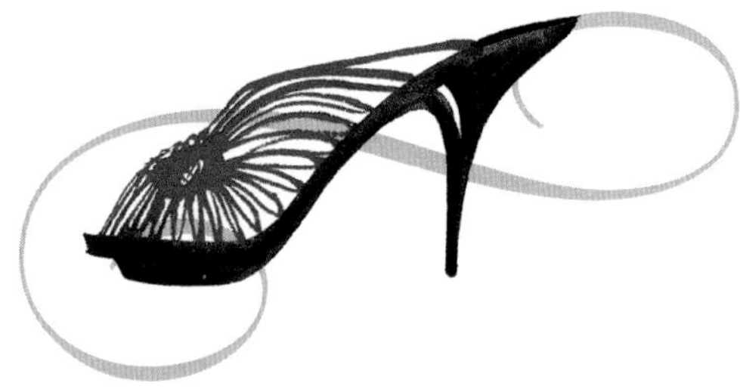

The BIG DATE. So exciting. And nerve-racking! Butterflies in the belly and playful fantasies on the mind. You want to laugh and cry, and you want a guarantee of a good hair night and no surprise blemishes. The first date is romantic and thrilling all at once. First dates (dates in general, really) are one of the things I miss most about being single. And hands down, dressing for a first date is one thousand times more complicated than dressing for a job interview, though they're not entirely different—a first date is a sort of job interview for a relationship. If I added up the many hours I've spent rummaging through my closet looking for that perfect outfit, I'd have a whole month of leisure time. At least! Your ensemble always sends a myriad of subtle signals, and on a first date (especially if it's with someone you really like) you must balance them flawlessly.

> *The best thing is to look natural,*
> *but it takes makeup to look natural.*
>
> CALVIN KLEIN

YOUR OUTFIT SHOULD SAY, I AM . . .

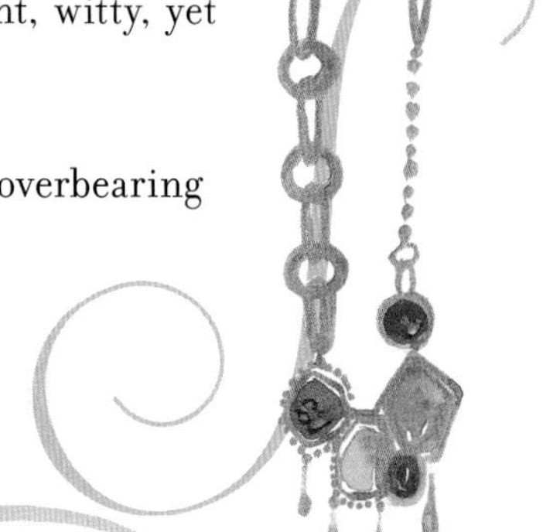

- Heart-stoppingly beautiful, intelligent, witty, yet low maintenance
- Mysterious yet totally approachable
- Sexy and confident, yet not tarty and overbearing
- Tasteful but not boring
- Fun but not flaky
- Arty but not pretentious
- Cerebral but not too scholarly
- Laid back but not frumpy

Your ensemble has to be subtle, sexy, and smart. It has to say everything while looking like you just threw it together without a thought. Easy, right?

It can be.

If he's arranged the date, listen carefully to the details so you can plan your outfit accordingly. If you aren't familiar with the restaurant he's chosen, undertake your own covert operation and find out as much as you can about the tone of the place. Google it, ask friends who've been there, and if you're still not sure how formal to go, call the restaurant and ask if men are required to wear a tie, as this will give you a clue as to how formal or informal the place is. And ladies, a bit of advice: Going dutch right away sets a bad precedent. If you invited him out you *can* pay; however, as a rule he should pick up the check on the first date. If he's a class act he'll insist on it.

First impressions are generated in the amygdala, the most primitive part of the brain where feelings are processed, so it is crucial that you make the best first impression possible. Looking gorgeous has less to do with genetics than it does with knowing how to make the most of your assets while minimizing your problem areas. Knowing you look amazing gives you a surge of confidence—which is more flattering than any garment in existence. I am sure all of us know a woman with a wonderful husband or boyfriend who doesn't look like a Victoria's Secret model, she isn't always the most chicly turned out woman in the room, and she doesn't wear head-to-toe designer clothes. But she always lands the right man. What's her secret? Confidence. Self-confidence is supremely attractive to men.

rule breakers we love

Jane Birkin

Singer, model, actress, muse. Jane Birkin is all of these and more. How many women have an Hermès bag named after them? Jane does, because she's truly unique. The bangs, the superminis, those eyes. . . . We should all aspire to be as extraordinary.

The Look of Seduction

I'm very often asked what my ideal first date outfit is, most likely because women feel so much anxiety around dating, and we have all had at least one at some point in our lives. There are so many instances where a specific item just isn't appropriate. I would never wear a miniskirt to a bowling alley, although if a guy wanted to take me to a bowling alley on a first date, I may rethink the whole thing entirely. So let's take the stock "dinner" as the first date destination, and work from there. On such an excursion, I would keep it cool and simple with a pretty, flowy dress, nipped in at the waist. Choose something in a soft, natural fabric that lightly hugs your curves.

You want your date to remember *you*, not your straight-off-the-runway Gucci ensemble, so don't wear anything too trendy. Fashion is meant to complement your personality and enhance it, but never rule over your personal style. Choose a color that plays up your complexion, hair, and eyes. Keep the focus on you by avoiding overly bright or neon colors. Try burgundy instead of fire engine red, or pink instead of fuchsia. Remember it's all about subtlety, mystery, romance. Add a glamorous touch of color with a silk scarf.

I know it's tempting to run out and buy a brand-new outfit for a first date. We all get a little rush of excitement at the prospect of going shopping for something special, but this is not the time. You're much better off wearing clothes, shoes especially, that you've already tested. Looking as if you were born to wear your clothes comes from actually wearing them and getting to know them. Comfort must be first and foremost in your mind. Can you comfortably sit in what you're wearing? Can you dance in it? How is it best accessorized? All of these questions must be answered before you can confidently embody the fierceness of your ensemble.

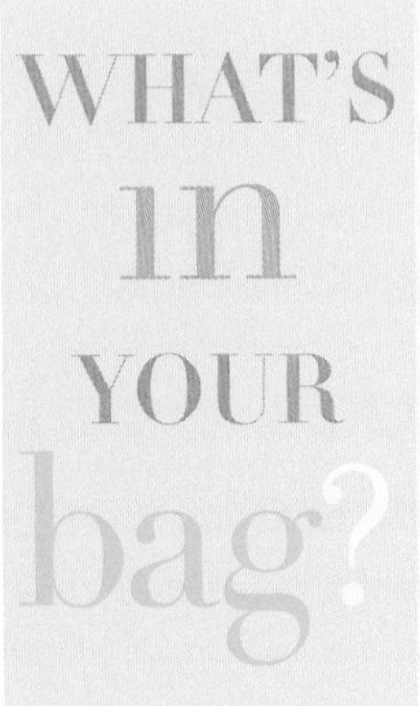

Unless you're secretly planning to escape to Rio, don't carry an enormous tote bag on a first date. This is a pet peeve of mine. There is no reason for a woman to be all dressed up, carrying a huge designer bag. It detracts from everything else she has on and, worse, it creates the illusion that she's large. No one wants that. Opt for a small clutch. All you need to bring on a dinner date are lipstick, some powder, your wallet, and a mirror. Don't forget to toss in some mints!

Your style goal for a first date is to be effortlessly cool and sexy. If you feel it, he will too. What looks great is usually what makes you feel comfortable. You do not want to be shivering cold or complaining that you can't walk in your shoes. You've got to feel at ease. No tight corsets that restrict your breathing. No Spanx digging into your skin. As long as you feel like a force of nature, you will have a spectacular night.

Let's be realistic, most guys have pretty conservative taste; they don't want a girlfriend who dresses like she may run off with the first new guy she sees. If that *is* what your date likes, I would reevaluate going out with him in the first place.

Clothes That Boys Understand

- NATURAL: Natural makeup AND natural hair. Ask any man, and he'll tell you that he finds a woman most beautiful first thing in the morning, fresh-faced and sleepy.
- FITTED OR SKINNY JEANS: Nothing is more alluring to a man than a woman who looks good in her jeans—and knows it.
- A NICE FITTED TOP, TEE, V-NECK SWEATER: Don't show too much, keep them guessing.
- A SIMPLE DRESS THAT IS TAILORED AND FEMININE, NOT TOO TIGHT OR SHORT: See above.
- LITTLE HEELS, BOOTS, OR FLATS: Stilettos look phenomenal but they can seem a bit dangerous and might prove overwhelming for the first date.

FIRST DATE *DON'TS*

- Avoid anything too short, tight, or shiny.
- No navel-baring décolletage. Mystery is a powerful aphrodisiac.
- No animal prints.
- No piercings. Piercings can be a bit scary for the first date, depending on his style.
- No long, bright nails. Talons aren't sexy.
- Don't drape yourself in jewels and baubles. Men are leery of excessive trimming.

I used to tremble from nerves so badly that the only way I could hold my head steady was to lower my chin practically to my chest and look up at Bogie.
That was the beginning of The Look.

LAUREN BACALL

Now that you've chosen an outfit, you must assess it bluntly in front of a mirror or model it for a good friend. Make sure she's a very, very good friend. What message does it convey? I know you are probably hoping for sexy siren, but don't take it too far. While it is tempting to try to put together a look that's straight from a magazine spread, remember that those photos are staged; in real life there's a very fine line between sexy and stripper. Beware and go for demure. You can have fun later, I promise.

Take your time getting ready for the big night. Your entire look must be completely put together, and in a seemingly carefree manner, before the date begins. There's nothing more distracting than the nagging feeling that you need to check your hair and makeup every ten minutes when you should really be paying attention to the early, subtle signs of pending love. You want to be able to showcase your true self, and not the self that's wondering if she has lipstick on her teeth.

Before you take the leap into that incomparable first-date sea of awkwardness and romance, stop and reflect on your FIRST EVER first date. Evoke this openhearted spirit when you're getting ready for any date. He will find the combination of your flushed cheeks and the subtle undercurrent of anticipation irresistible. It will be up to you to decide if you want a second date or not. And there's nothing sweeter than the curious crush that starts to simmer with the promise of that second date. Such possibilities!

Now, the outfit options I describe are *my* ideal first date outfit, but remember, whatever you wear should make *you* feel vibrant and irresistible. If you are a rocker babe, do not show up in Laura Ashley just to please him. Do not break the bank buying designer brands to impress him. I assure you he will not know the difference. If he does, you might have a problem . . .

Your coif should be done/undone. Tousled, not frizzy or messy, with a hint of "I just rolled out of bed." No tight buns, ladies!

A first date is all about the face. Your date will be gazing over the table at you, so look pretty. As a rule, it's best to keep your makeup natural; you want it to hold up for the entire evening. However, the most important thing is to stay true to yourself, so if your look is dramatic 24/7, with a heavy lip and eye, go for it. Just don't overdo it; you don't want to look scary. If you think you'll want a good night kiss, avoid deep red lipstick—some men find it a bit intimidating. Remember, natural; this is not the Academy Awards (unless you're a very lucky woman). If you know you *don't* want that kiss good night so soon, then rock a deep crimson lip. The color is sexy, but also says, "Approach with caution."

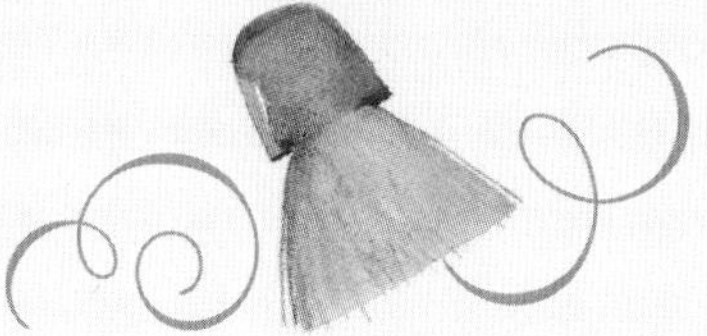

And the Beat Goes On

What to Wear on a Casual Date (or Any Date After the First Date)

My ideas for this look sparked quite a debate among some of my girlfriends. So let me clarify what I mean by "casual date." I'm referring to any date after the first, but BEFORE you are officially a couple. This is the priceless stage when everything is still pristine and exciting. You still get nervous before you see him, and you count the days between his phone calls. When he texts you, you still get a shiver as you read a message as inane as "hello." And anytime you hear the ping that signals you do have a new text, you hope that it's him, and are incredibly disappointed when it's not. Yet with each date, the two of you are getting more comfortable being together.

Style-wise this period is extra fun because every outfit you put on is new to him (even if he doesn't notice the outfit, it'll give you a little extra sparkle that he will notice). These dates are filled with sexual tension; the tingling in your stomach nearly drives you mad; you fall asleep with a smile on your face and awake smiling the next morning. This is crazy! This is life. Treasure these dates.

There are an endless number of date scenarios, but I'm going to stick with the basics here. Adjust the following to fit your specific activity, if you can.

> *The average man is more interested in a woman who is interested in him than he is in a woman with beautiful legs.*
>
> MARLENE DIETRICH

Dinner and a Movie

On such an excursion, I would keep it cool and simple with a great pair of jeans that I know look amazing on me. I mean THE jeans that fit perfectly. High-heel boots or booties go with everything, so I would wear whichever I'm feeling that evening, or whichever works best with the rest of my look. I live in high heels; those added vertical inches make me feel powerful, but if you don't wear heels often, put on what makes you feel great. Boots are the perfect blend of casual and sexy, and I find the rhythmic click of heels on pavement alluring and feminine. However, make sure to wear shoes that you can actually walk in, so you can enjoy a leisurely stroll if things go well. Also slip on a loose, soft, and silky top that shows just a hint of cleavage and enhances your curves beautifully, or something off the shoulder, which is always tantalizing. And finish the look with a leather jacket. Leather is sensual and just dangerous enough.

This outfit will take you anywhere—from dinner, to drinks, to dancing, to a movie, to a concert, and yes, even bowling, you name it. It's fabulously, classically all-purpose. Your date will fall in love. It worked like a charm on my husband.

But if jeans aren't your first choice, and for some of us they just aren't, try a denim pencil skirt instead. The look is very sexy, but it still maintains the casual nonchalance of jeans. Another option that works wonderfully is a colorful sheath paired with subtle patterned tights and booties.

Take the DNA of what we discussed in our First Date chapter, and mold it so that it's a bit more relaxed and comfortable. It's just dinner and a movie, for goodness sake! Remember to think about what's appropriate. A movie theater is not the best place to showcase your micromini; we've all seen what can happen when you're exiting a car.

And please don't hog the popcorn.

rule breakers we love

Charlotte Gainsbourg

Actress and singer-songwriter, she is that perfect combination of gamine, indie rock, and French flair. Her long, brown, always perfectly tousled hair, with long bangs almost falling into her eyes, complements her easy, laid-back wardrobe. So sexy, so cool.

Dinner at a Restaurant

This date is one you can get dressed up for. Easy style takes a backseat to shimmer and glam for this kind of romantic evening. Fine dining with a handsome date is like being in a scene from an old film; it's your moment to shine. There are few things more visually enticing than a beautiful woman dressed for a fabulous dinner. It's the stuff songs are written about.

Be elegant, but also walk the edge. It's the perfect time for stilettos, if you wear them—sometimes the pain is worth looking and feeling like the most glamorous girl in the restaurant. Besides, a fancy dinner usually means you'll be traveling in his car or a taxi, so make the sacrifice and whip out the stunning shoes. Show a hint of cleavage with a neckline that's just a tad lower than your everyday look. Enhance your curves with a dress or pant that hugs them a little more snugly than usual. Think about your silhouette and aim for hourglass. A slight caress of fabric around your body will make you feel extra special, and give you a glamorous aura.

A cocktail ring and/or subtly glittering earrings are definitely welcome accessories for a night out. The key words here are glitz, wine, gourmet decadence, and good company. Toast to that.

Casual Drinks

This date is deceptive. You might think it takes less planning than the others, but that is not the case. Think of this occasion as two notches down from your restaurant look. Wear something edgier, like a leather motorcycle jacket paired with your silk blouse and cool trousers. Or if you're feeling a bit girlier, try a dress under your motorcycle jacket, with boots. A smoky eye and higher heel will give you a mysteriously powerful edge.

> *A girl with brains ought to*
> *do something with them besides think.*
>
> GENTLEMEN PREFER BLONDES

What every woman must remember when dressing for a casual date is HE LIKES YOU and HE THINKS YOU'RE GORGEOUS. Otherwise, he wouldn't have asked you out again. So be confident. Insecurity is a terrible fashion faux pas. Your style comes from within, and fashion is just the icing on the scrumptious cake that is you and only you. You always want to come across as appropriate, but this isn't a stuffy job interview. It's OK to push the envelope when it comes to dressing for love.

Wear lingerie that's meant to be seen, even if he won't see it. Wearing something sexy underneath translates into feeling that way. You are a woman—inside and out. This is a great time in the relationship to have fun with lingerie. Splurge on a beautiful, luxurious silk bra and gorgeous stockings. Anything with lace is always fantastic. Go for La Perla, Agent Provocateur, Parah.

Ode to Cozy

What to Wear for a Netflix Night In

I can't think of a more enjoyable, cozy, and relaxing way to spend an evening than snuggling up at home to watch a movie with my husband. Don't get me wrong, I adore dressing up and going out, but balance is key in every area of life, and all women should find that perfect harmony between slipping on your highest heels and staying home and ordering in. Lying low and cuddling is a core component in every relationship. Queue up Netflix, see what's On Demand, and relax. You're in for the night. Now what the hell do you wear?

Even though you won't have to face the public tonight, and even though a night in with your man indicates the relationship has reached a *certain* level of intimacy, you don't want to look entirely like you've been snowed in for a month, or worse, like someone who has been studying for her LSATs. You've got to keep that spark lit. This means *never* wearing a Snuggie. This is not the night to vamp it up either. Doing so would create the entirely wrong mood for a relaxing evening. A woman in jeans and a T-shirt, all fresh-faced with her hair undone, is incredibly sexy. Jessica Biel is the poster girl for this type of gorgeous, rough-and-tumble, easy beauty.

> *My idea of heaven is a great big baked potato, and someone to share it with.*
>
> OPRAH WINFREY

KEEP THE ENVIRONMENT SEXY

- LIGHT SOME CANDLES FOR A COZY VIBE. Some of my favorites are Aedes de Venustas. If you're in a mysterious and exotic mood, try a Baies candle by Diptyque; or for a fresh, green scent try Verte by Vie Luxe. Even better, light a fire if you have a fireplace.
- ENJOY A GOOD BOTTLE OF WINE. Wine goes with everything.
- HAVE MUSIC READY to keep the ambiance going after the movie ends. This is a crucial shift in the evening. Be prepared.
- FLUFF UP YOUR PILLOWS. It refreshes the energy in the room.

It's actually rather amazing that we don't need to leave the house anymore for dinner and a movie. Many of you may remember the days of trudging to the video store, hoping the flick you've chosen isn't already checked out, and settling on one you're not sure about instead. Today everything is one or two clicks away on your computer—dinner *and* the movie. You can coordinate your entire date from the comfort of your home.

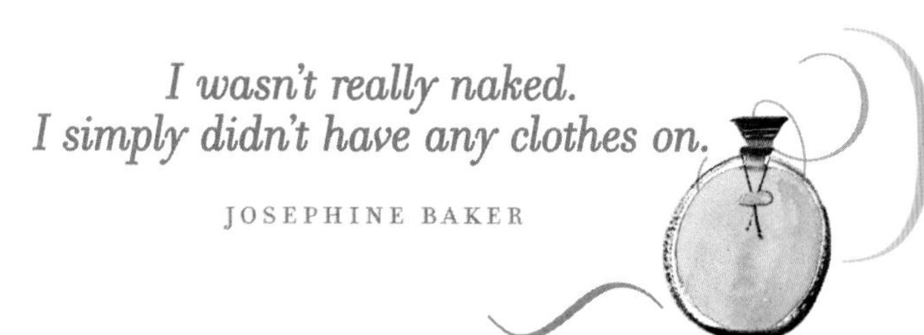

> *I wasn't really naked.*
> *I simply didn't have any clothes on.*
>
> JOSEPHINE BAKER

Wear whatever you feel best in on this night. Jeans are ideal. Sweats are OK too (but they must be adorable). Fabric is of the utmost importance; keep it soft with natural fibers like a light cotton or cashmere. The point is to be at ease, sensual, and as natural as possible. It's all about what feels good to touch and be close to. Wear his oversize shirt or a cozy, cotton-knit shirt with leggings. Lounge in style and slip on a silk robe over silk pajamas or maybe a sumptuous silk caftan. Anything that feels luxurious against your skin is irresistible to him.

If you're lucky enough to look fabulous sans makeup, by all means go au naturel. Though a little lip gloss never hurt anyone.

UNDERNEATH it all

NAUGHTY OR NICE?

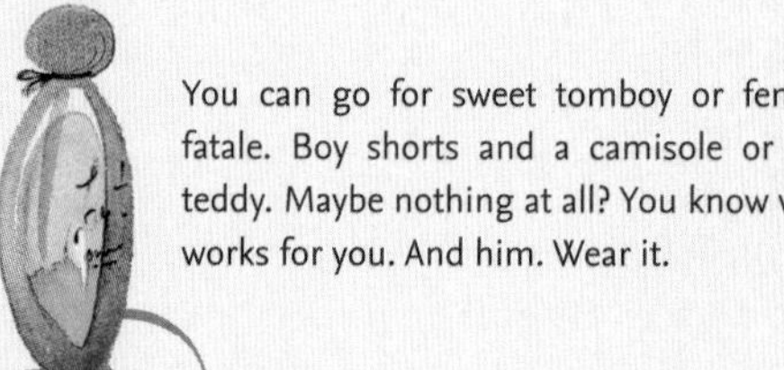

You can go for sweet tomboy or femme fatale. Boy shorts and a camisole or lace teddy. Maybe nothing at all? You know what works for you. And him. Wear it.

Love Hurts—Style Shouldn't

What to Wear When You Break Up with Your Boyfriend

There are situations in life that we would all love to avoid—moments when we'd rather not answer any text messages or phone calls, and when we'd love to chuck our to-do list into a blazing fire. But our very desire to avoid this sort of situation is often a sign that it is something that *must* be taken care of. It's best to face this sort of awkward occasion head-on. Sometimes, confrontation is necessary. And breaking it off with someone is one of these treacherous moments.

If your boyfriend was a jerk and deserves to be heaved, having a loud breakup can be the best medicine for your feelings of betrayal and anger at yourself for ever falling hard for such a fool. And if your boyfriend was well meaning and sweet, but you're just not feeling what you need to feel for a successful relationship, your respectfulness toward him will have a positive effect on your own self-esteem. In either case, what do you wear?

> *I change my mind so much*
> *I need two boyfriends and a girlfriend.*
>
> PINK

It actually does matter. Think of it this way: The most important thing you want to communicate in the midst of love tribulation is that you are not a victim; you are a woman making a critical choice. Your look needs to reflect your strength. Your ensemble should be appropriate, with just

enough solemnity to match the sentiment of romantic disengagement. However, if your soon-to-be-ex has been a jerk, you also want to remind him of your inherent, God-given hotness; you want him to see, one last time, what he will be missing and appreciate what he had. Stylistically, it's a delicate balance, but it's totally doable.

If you're the one doing the breaking up and if he is a nice guy, just the wrong nice guy, then understated, even bordering on austere, is a good way to go. Wear an outfit that shows you DO take this seriously, and that you know something very special has come to an end. You might choose something dark, perhaps steely gray, to match your resolve; or you might be the kind of girl who wears a pretty little day dress to neutralize the negative aura. Just don't let the crisis factor become an excuse for looking less than perfect. You want him to remember just how amazing you are. More important, you want to remind *yourself* of this critical fact.

This probably goes without saying, but don't accessorize with jewelry that he's given you. It's just bad form, unless you *want* to make a statement. I personally wouldn't. Karma does exist. That said, if the bastard cheated on you, wear his favorite dress, the jewelry he gave you, and make him cry.

> *The minute you settle for less than you deserve, you get even less than you settled for.*
>
> MAUREEN DOWD

rule breakers we love

Salome

Salome was a dangerous heartbreaker. You don't need to take it as far as using your wiles to cause a murder, but it might not hurt to learn the Dance of the Seven Veils for your next boyfriend.

Where Will It All End?

Many people, especially those of the male persuasion, seem to believe it's better to break up in a public setting, perhaps over drinks or dinner. The idea is to minimize drama, because you're not supposed to feel comfortable enough in public to start crying or yelling, or both. A good rule of thumb for the public breakup as the prime venue of choice is, if you've been together less than six months, it's OK. At this stage, there really hasn't been enough time for either of you to feel like the world would end if the relationship ended. Still difficult, mind you, but fireworks? Probably not. If you've been together any longer than a year, talk in private; this shows respect for the relationship you shared.

In most cases, you need to stick to your guns once you've come this far, no matter how hard he tries to change your mind. Don't back down because you feel bad—no one wants a relationship based on pity.

THE coif THE face

Consider pulling your hair back into a very sleek ponytail. Don't put on too much makeup. This is a time to show him you're being honest about how you feel, and that ending the relationship is the route you've chosen. There's no going back.

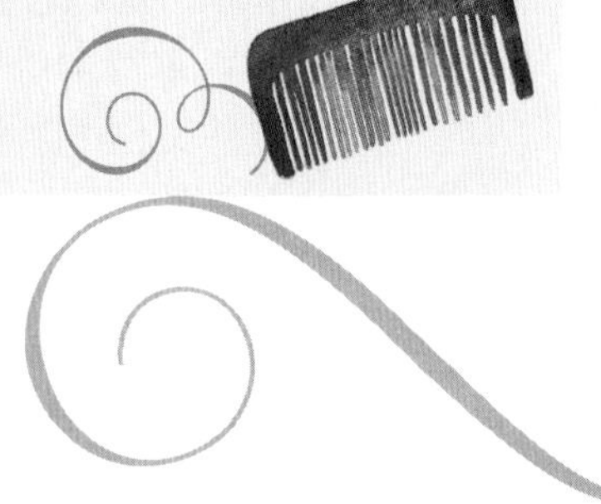

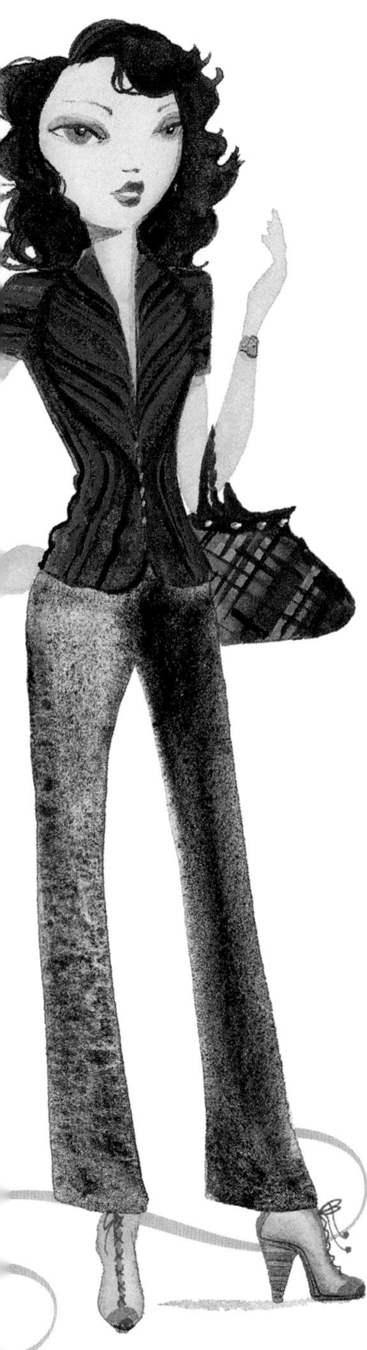

Shopping Around

What to Wear on a Blind Date

Blind dates can be frightening. I know a woman who literally started twitching at the prospect of being set up on a blind date. Why do we all dread them? Two fears almost inevitably come up: rejection and . . . repulsion. Every woman really should go on at least one blind date in her lifetime, though. Yes, nine times out of ten they're a horror show, but you'll have a good story to tell, and ultimately it does build character. A bad blind date will make you think twice about playing Cupid yourself. And a terrible date can teach you a lot about what you *don't* want in a man. If fortune smiles on you and you hit it off, congratulations. Either way, savor the experience from start to finish. Bask in the thrill of the unknown—consider that dating is just another word for networking—and revel in the anticipation that you may be meeting the man of your dreams. However, always keep one fabulous heel firmly planted on the ground.

Blind dates are usually fairly casual, quick drinks or dinner, so you don't need to worry about getting too dressed up. Since you have no idea what to expect, there's less pressure to look your best than on a first date with a man that you *really* hope will like you. On the flipside, what if he is amazing? There is nothing worse than showing up to a blind date with that bored and cocky you're-lucky-I'm-even-taking-the-time-to-meet-you attitude, only to discover that the man in question is not only hot, but incredibly cool. You'll wish you had cared just a little bit more.

I have been on a few blind dates myself, and let me tell you, it takes only one long, uncomfortable evening with Mr. Wrong to learn you should always have an exit strategy in your back pocket. Just in case. I recommend meeting for drinks. If all goes well, you can move on to dinner. If he's clearly a dud, down your drink, make your excuses, and run home to lecture whoever set you up on what exactly your type is, so this never happens again.

> *To find a prince, you gotta kiss some toads.*
>
> FOXY BROWN

What You Should Wear

TROUSERS: Tailored black trousers or slouchy peg legs.
SHIRT: A V-neck knit with capped sleeves, a generous shawl collar, and a diagonal stripe. A chevron stripe is extremely slimming. Instant hourglass figure.
JACKET: A cool cropped motorcycle jacket or a sleek trench.
SHOES: Stacked-heel booties, Mary Janes, ballet flats.
ACCESSORIES: Nothing shows off a woman's bare arm to perfection like a gorgeous cuff bracelet. A cuff makes you feel like a warrior. Repeat this mantra before you leave the house: "I am a powerful, confident woman with a lot to offer. I deserve a wonderful man."

FEMALE ARCHETYPES MEN LOVE

The Bombshell

- BRIGITTE BARDOT: The ultimate sex kitten—spectacular and confident in a bikini, with her cat-eye liner and tousled hair.
- SOPHIA LOREN: The dark beauty. Her strength and passion are magnetic.
- SCARLETT JOHANSSON: She's the modern (sometimes blond) bombshell. She celebrates her femininity and her curves.

The Class Act

- GRACE KELLY: The tall, cool blonde. She was just unapproachable enough to drive men wild.
- AUDREY HEPBURN: The ultimate gamine beauty. She was striking yet soft, chic yet tomboyish.
- REESE WITHERSPOON: A modern Grace Kelly. Talented and knows how to get what she wants while always remaining a lady.

The Femme Fatale

- CLEOPATRA: The iconic kohl eyeliner. She was exotic and powerful, and men still fantasize about her.
- GILDA: Rita Hayworth embodied Gilda's fearless, slightly selfish sexuality. That she was bad news only made men want her more.
- ANGELINA JOLIE: She's strong and independent, and if she wants a man, she gets him.

One of the Boys

- KATHARINE HEPBURN: She was gorgeous and had swagger. Witty banter is the best foreplay.
- JEAN SEBERG: Her sexy, paperboy pixie cut drove Jean-Paul Belmondo (and every other man on the planet) wild.
- CAMERON DIAZ: She's sporty, bubbly, and gorgeous. Just the sort of girl men love to relax and hang out with.

What to Wear After You've Been Cruelly Dumped

Getting dumped. It's the worst. We've all been there. If you haven't, you are unbelievably lucky and I just might hate you. For the rest of us mere mortals, this is a very, very difficult time. There's a mourning period—you go through the stages of grief: denial, anger, bargaining, depression, and, at long last, acceptance. For at least a week you don't want to change out of your sweats, much less leave the house. You sit there with your hair piled onto your head in a messy bun, and you listen to the song that reminds you of him one too many times each morning. Give yourself a break and allow yourself to wallow, for a very limited period of time.

WHAT'S in YOUR bag?

- **PRETTY TISSUES:** It's a small thing, but wiping your tears with a well-designed tissue helps; you need to surround yourself with beauty.
- **VITAMIN PACKS:** You've got to keep your strength up and your skin glowing.
- **SUNGLASSES:** When you're prone to crying jags, you will look tremendously chic in an oversize pair of Jackie O's.
- **MINTS:** Crying jags can lead to less-than-fresh breath.
- **XANAX:** Use only in extreme cases, like being left at the altar.
- **RED LIPSTICK:** Express your powerful femininity with a bold color.

PHOENIXES

- PRINCESS DIANA: She came through one of the most public divorces in history smelling like the beautiful English rose she was.
- DEBBIE REYNOLDS: She's got spirit, talent, and gams. Who needs Eddie Fisher?
- JENNIFER ANISTON: I don't think there's another woman in the world who has had to endure more tabloid photos of her ex and his new family. She is a class act.
- NICOLE KIDMAN: It is to her credit that we don't know what led to her divorce from Tom Cruise. She's never said a bad word about him in public.
- SIENNA MILLER: She survived the worst cliché around (catching the nanny and her fiancé) with true panache.

> *When you're feeling blue,*
> *think red.*
>
> PAULINE TRIGÈRE

> *A friend will tell you she saw your old boyfriend—and he's a priest.*
>
> ERMA BOMBECK

When you are finally ready to venture out, you probably won't care about what you look like. You will never love anyone again, much less date, so what's the point of trying to be pretty? Sound familiar? But Murphy's Law ensures that even if your ex lives in another state, he will magically be at your grocery store at the precise moment you drag yourself out of your house—in the sweats you slept in, with bags under your eyes, and that sad bun on your head—to replenish your supply of wine, Kleenex, and ice cream. I realize that you won't be able to muster your fiercest look, but you can appear presentable without too much effort, and the process of putting that look together might even make you feel better.

STYLE THERAPY FOR BROKEN HEARTS

- Find a flirty, sexy new fragrance for the flirty, sexy new you.
- Splurge on a new pair of beautiful and expensive high heels—sometimes you need a little shopping therapy. These are for the forthcoming dates you'll be going on.
- Wear a charm bracelet or a cocktail ring; costume or real, it doesn't matter as long as it sparkles when you gesture. And while you're at it, indulge in a manicure too!
- Treat yourself to an espresso or latte and luxuriate in the caffeinated goodness.
- Get a brand-new "do." Try a fresh cut or style, or just brighten your look up with some highlights.
- Wallow to anything by Patsy Cline or Billie Holiday, then move

on to anything by Mazzy Star or Anita O'Day. (Eventually you'll snap out of it, throw on some Bob Marley, and rise up.)

- Take baby steps at first. You may be the only person who sees them, but put on a pair of sexy panties anyway and pair them with a pretty, girlie bra. It helps, really.
- Last, and definitely not least, relish in the one awesome result of a bad breakup: weight loss. Take advantage and hit the gym to revitalize your body and spirit. You'll have shed those five pounds by the time your heart is mended and you'll be back in your skinny jeans, looking fab and on the prowl.

After you've been cruelly dumped, you are like a delicate flower. Your fragile ego needs to be nurtured and coaxed into bloom. You have to make yourself feel pretty and you have to pull yourself together enough to make your ex (should you run into him) feel a pang of regret. Most important, if you *look* fierce every time you go out, before you know it you will *feel* fierce. Best-case scenario: You'll never run into your ex and your outer fabulosity will speed the healing process. Worst-case scenario: You'll see a little glint in his eye as you sail by him with a dismissive nod, knowing what a fool he was. You are so much better than he is anyway.

The New Crew

What to Wear to Meet Your New Boyfriend's Friends

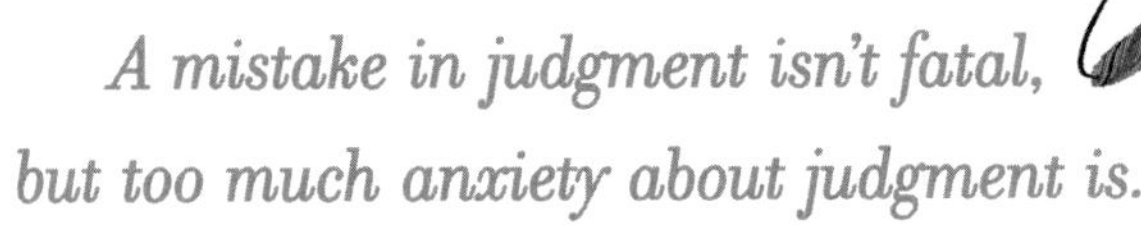

A mistake in judgment isn't fatal, but too much anxiety about judgment is.

PAULINE KAEL

There is a lot of pressure the first time your new boyfriend introduces you to his inner circle. If he is sensitive and kind, he'll work you slowly into his crowd rather than springing them all on you at once. It'll be difficult to tune out the little voices in your head, reminding you his friends know everyone he's dated before; that they may still be in touch with one or more of his exes; that you're probably being compared to girlfriends past; and that you may even have to contend with that one female friend who secretly loves him (which he's oblivious to). *My Best Friend's Wedding* springs to mind. Tune out those voices. Your boyfriend adores you. You know this because he's introducing you to his friends. The only real threat to your relationship is your nagging insecurity about meeting these people. And what better way to dispel that insecurity than to create the perfect outfit?

Fashion can be an excellent over-the-counter anti-anxiety drug.

Center yourself. It's going to be OK. Put together an outfit that communicates subtle layers of confidence and friendliness, while also looking fabulous. You can do it. Meeting his friends usually takes place at a party, over drinks or dinner, or at some other fairly laid-back social event. With this in mind, I'm going to assume the dress code is evening casual. This takes a huge load off, so you can focus more clearly on your main objective, which is to connect with a group of people who you might be spending a lot of time with down the line. Make it matter.

What You Should Wear

JEANS: Denim is a great combination of cool, friendly, and easy. And guys can relate to denim; it's a familiar and nonthreatening look. Silly but true. Also, other women at the party are less likely to get catty if you dress down a bit and wear jeans. I don't know why this is, but it's what I've seen; the opposite is true if you wear a dress. Your style goal is friendly and approachable.

TOP: Wear a top that looks great on you but isn't too revealing. You want to connect with his friends, not distract them with your cleavage. Also, again, he may get uncomfortable if he notices his friends checking you out.

SHOES: Boots or booties. Whenever I'm going somewhere that I know may be intimidating, I try to wear platforms. Height is a confidence builder. Meeting your new boyfriend's posse calls for a chunky or wedge heel; you get the height without the stiletto's too sexy look.

BAG: Nothing with logos, I hope. You don't want to look like a material girl, just a cool girl.

COLOR: Choose something positive and approachable. You don't want to be in head-to-toe black unless you live in New York City.

rule breakers we love

Slim Keith

Dubbed the original "California girl," she embodied cool, sophisticated style. When Slim, Babe Paley, and Truman Capote hit the town, everyone in New York knew about it the next day.

MEETING THE NEW BOYFRIEND'S POSSE *DON'TS*

- DON'T DRAPE YOURSELF IN JEWELS. The guy friends in particular will read this as high maintenance. Even if you are high maintenance, you don't want it to be their first impression of you.
- AVOID PLUNGING NECKLINES AND MICROMINIS. You're already gorgeous; you don't need to flaunt it. And you don't want to make your new boyfriend uncomfortable.
- DON'T MONOPOLIZE THE CONVERSATION IN AN ATTEMPT TO IMPRESS. Everyone loves a good listener.

The important thing is not what they think of me, but what I think of them.

QUEEN VICTORIA

THE ZEN PATH TO A GOOD IMPRESSION

- Peace and tranquility will conquer all.
- Take a morning yoga class.
- Burn some sage.
- Call your best friend for a pre-outing pep talk.
- Make a list of what you love about your boyfriend, and remember that list if anything gets too awkward.
- Don't try too hard. Remember, they are the ones who are lucky to meet you—and not the other way around.
- Make your boyfriend proud. Be the girl he fell in love with.
- Smile. Always smile.

Staking Claim

What to Wear to Meet Your Boyfriend's Ex

Don't you wish your girlfriend was hot like me?

PUSSYCAT DOLLS

Running into your new boyfriend's ex is usually a spontaneous and somewhat horrifying event that, unfortunately, most of us have zero opportunity to plan for. However, if you are forewarned and can plan for it, my best advice is to stay strong. He's yours. You know this. Above all, resist the urge to be catty—when you start putting others down, those negative thoughts inevitably turn inward, and that only makes you more insecure. Concentrate on yourself; accentuate the positive.

This encounter with the ex will probably occur around something that is considered an errand, such as picking up or dropping off children, or attending a function hosted by mutual friends. Odds are formal attire will not be required. Whatever the occasion, however, the outfit you wear needs to make you KNOW you look good. You have to ooze confidence. This is no time for experimentation. Don't debut that brand-new dress. Don't wear the top you're still a bit unsure of. Don't do something drastic with your hair that very afternoon! You'll regret it.

What You Should Wear
If the Encounter Happens at a Party

DRESS: Wear your sexiest dress, the one that makes you feel and look like a million bucks. An A-line skirt or dress is always fun and fashionable.

SHOES: High, high, high. Height is power—as long as you can stride with confidence. Wear your most fabulous Louis Vuittons. You'll feel tall, willowy, and the total woman your man adores.

DON'T WORRY, BE HAPPY

- Radiate self-confidence from every pore of your body. Prepare for, but don't obsess over this meeting.
- Meditate. Clear your mind and just breathe.
- If you're showing any skin, make sure it's glowing. Exfoliate and super moisturize for several days beforehand. Nothing is sexier than great skin—nothing.
- Make your smile dazzle. Consider some muted bleaching, emphasis on muted—you're trying to dazzle, not blind.
- Cleanse. Victoria's Secret models cleanse for a few days prior to an event. Your skin will look fabulous and so will your figure.
- Use aromatherapy. Take a bath and light some scented candles. Lavender is extra calming.
- Have a glass of wine.
- Listen to your favorite music and get your mojo going.
- Remind yourself that you are an adult capable of facing anything.
- Seal it with a kiss. Take half an hour or so for a make-out session with your current boyfriend beforehand. You'll be surrounded in a bubble of kiss-afterglow.

> *Whenever you want to marry someone, go have lunch with his ex-wife.*
>
> SHELLEY WINTERS

The trick to effortless is keeping the trimming to a minimum. Edit. Edit. Edit. Understated glamour is the goal here. Add a little glitter, but don't whip out the entire jewelry box. Wear something he gave you. You'll get a little boost every time someone compliments your treasure. Feel beautiful, be beautiful, and remember, he's there with you. And he's a damn lucky man.

Before you know it, the dreaded first meeting with the ex will be a thing of the past and your relationship will have survived unscathed. Give yourself a well-deserved pat on the back for handling it with grace and aplomb. And exhale.

Hair and makeup should echo the tone of your outfit—flawless but never overdone. Your look should appear effortless; you don't want to seem like you are trying too hard.

The Moment of Impact

What to Wear When Meeting Your Significant Other's Parents

I told my mother-in-law that my house was her house, and she said, "Get the hell off my property."

JOAN RIVERS

There is nothing more nerve-racking than meeting your boyfriend's parents. Making a bad first impression on the parents (future in-laws even) can haunt your relationship for years to come. Making a great first impression turns this meeting into an exhilarating next step that brings you and your boyfriend even closer. No matter how likable and open-minded they are, they will be somewhat protective of their son. They're parents, it's their job. Show that you respect them and truly care for their son by looking your most ladylike and appealing best. As always, the most ladylike and appealing version of *you*, not who you imagine they want you to be. I will keep repeating this because it's so important to remember and so easy to forget. You must repeat it too.

It is a leap of faith to introduce one's past to one's present, with all that the meeting implies about one's future. All of this requires a certain level of trust—and depending on the state of his relationship with his parents, it could require an *enormous* amount of trust. Think of this as a modified job interview, but far more personal. You want to make a good impression; you want them to like you enough to have you around on a regular basis.

What do you want your ensemble to communicate? You should be respectful, open, ladylike, feminine, and, again, yourself. You want them to think you are a cut above the rest, but that doesn't mean you have to walk in wearing pearls and a twinset. It does, however, mean: no low back; no plunging décolletage; and no short hemlines. Wear something with sleeves, if possible, or bring along a beautiful scarf, or a cardigan (my favorite choice). Don't be afraid to be modern. Don't hold back the total woman that you have worked so hard to be. And take where you're going into consideration. Will this be a dinner at a formal restaurant, or a casual dinner at their house or your house, or will it be a group dinner? So many possibilities. It's hectic and stressful to try to cook dinner for his parents when first meeting them, so I highly recommend going out. Do your homework—get your boyfriend to give you as much info about their expectations as possible. If you know where they're coming from, you'll be ready to work your magic.

rule breakers we love

Clare Boothe Luce

She was a true Renaissance woman. Journalist, playwright, socialite, congresswoman, there wasn't anything she couldn't do. She was gorgeous, smart, talented, political, and so stylish. Invoke her spirit, always.

What You Should Wear

Don't wear anything too sexy. Be modest and go for warm earth tones or soft florals; both are inviting and grounded looks that say, "I'm smart and together."

SKIRT OR DRESS: An A-line skirt or dress with a knee-length hem is simple, easy, and flattering. Definitely no supermini here, ladies. Go for a simple sheath with clean lines and beautiful tailoring or a ladylike floral print with pleats or asymmetric draping. Think Alberta Ferretti, Chanel, or Prada.

TROUSERS: If you wear pants, opt for wide-leg smart trousers, and avoid tight pants or leggings. We are thinking conservative here.

BLOUSE: A beautiful scalloped blouse in a subtle print with some kind of feminine detail like soft ruffles or bows is modern, yet old-fashioned perfection.

SHOES: Wear low- to mid-heeled, classic pumps—something sleek and traditional like a Roger Vivier buckle shoe. Or pretty ballet flats.

BAG: No status handbags for this occasion; something classic and midsize will do.

ACCESSORIES: This is a good time to wear any of your sentimental family keepsakes. Your grandmother's pearls are beautifully classic and elegant. They reassure your boyfriend's mother that she has nothing to worry about. You have everything covered. If pearls aren't your style, think about wearing your mother's cameo or your school ring. If you don't own any family heirlooms, you can always find some vintage pieces that you like. It's all about personal jewelry, nothing flashy.

These situations are difficult for everyone, not just you. Be sure to compliment his mother on her outfit and laugh at his father's bad jokes. This advice may seem corny and old-fashioned, but it works!

The beauty who does not look surprised,
who accepts her position as her due—
she reminds us too much of a prima donna.

E. M. FORSTER

SET THE MOOD

Deep Breaths

- Choose the right time to meet the parents. Don't rush it. Wait until you're very comfortable with your boyfriend and let him bring it up.
- Ask your boyfriend to show you his baby pictures. Ooh and aah over what a cute baby he was.
- Be punctual. Remember, job interview. Not to mention it's very disrespectful to be late.
- Mind your manners. Brush up on your Emily Post etiquette and address everyone as "Sir" and "Mrs." Don't forget to say thank you. These little niceties go a long way.
- Even if it isn't a holiday, bring a small gift. Something simple like flowers, a scented candle, a book, a bottle of wine, or chocolates. They'll be on their way to falling in love with you.
- Be confident and self-assured. Go online and catch up on the latest headlines—parents love intelligent small talk (but stay away from religion and politics).
- Compliment the good food, their beautiful house. But don't go overboard; be genuine.
- Don't linger forever. Make a graceful exit when things are going well. Leave on a positive note and always leave them wanting more.

Unless you are going somewhere that's extremely informal, like an outdoor picnic, err on the formal side for this meeting. Embody the spirit of Julia Roberts or Cameron Diaz—they are both beautiful, independent women with quirky, winning personalities. Remember, meeting the parents is a two-way street; you're wooing EACH OTHER—they want to like you and they want you to like them.

You should keep your hair sleek and natural and your makeup to a minimum. Above all, be neat and well groomed.

Kid-Friendly Style

What to Wear When Meeting Your Significant Other's Children

Now this is a tough audience. The older we get, the more likely it is that there will be children in the dating mix. People get married, they have children, they get divorced. It happens. You may end up dating a man who's experienced all of this.

You must be ready.

Unfortunately, children are often predisposed to dislike anyone their father brings home who is not their mother, so you have your work cut out for you. On the plus side, some pressure is taken off by the fact that small children don't pay much attention to what you're wearing and teenagers think all adults look ridiculous anyway. If his kids are college-age or above, they will probably scrutinize your ensemble, but they're less likely to despise you on principle.

There are many variables involved with meeting your boyfriend's children, so in this case, it's all about your attitude. Be your funniest, most relaxed, playful self. Wear comfortable, carefree clothing if the kids are young—your favorite jeans, khakis, cargos. No intimidating outfits, just very real and laid-back. The less of a big deal you make about meeting them, the better.

> *Follow your bliss and the universe will open doors where there were only walls.*
>
> JOSEPH CAMPBELL

It's so important not to try too hard! Children, like chubby little bumblebees ready to strike, can smell desperation. These relationships take time, so don't push; don't feel bad if they don't love you immediately. Just be yourself, really listen to them, and treat them like the fascinating little individuals they are. They may be in your life for a very, very long time. Gradually show them how you will ultimately reign as Queen Bee.

If the children are standoffish, shrug it off. This isn't an easy thing to do—being snubbed by a child has an amazing ability to bring you right back to your own childhood. Suddenly you're worrying that you're a nerd and the popular kids are never going to accept you. Push away those feelings! You're an adult, their father thinks you're fabulous, and if you get to know them and allow them to get to know you, before you know it, you'll be friends and everything will turn out fine.

And guess what? You might just live happily ever after.

Now go watch some MTV, read all of the *Twilight* books, and watch a few episodes of *Degrassi: The Next Generation*. You'll need to have a full understanding of the tween/teenage mind. And remember, be comfortable and relaxed.

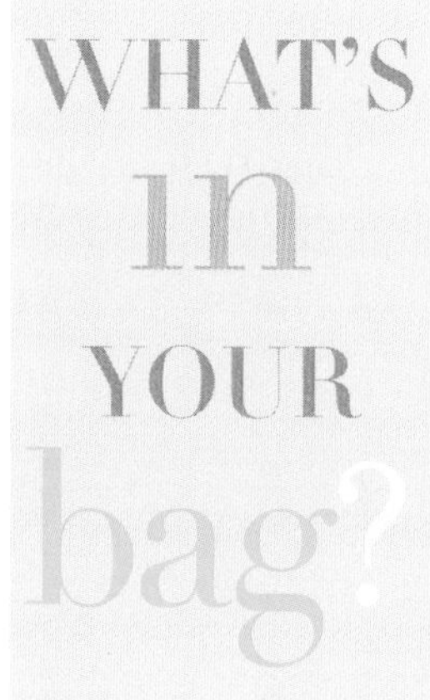

You're going to want some distractions. Throw in a magazine or some interesting gadgets to pull out in case of awkward silences. You'd be surprised at how easy it is to distract a baby with an iPhone. Why not carry a Slinky? Once on a table, it's irresistible to people of any age.

day

Task Mistress

What to Wear for a Day of Errands

Frumps are often celebrities in disguise—but a person of vulgar appearance is vulgar through and through.

FROM *ETIQUETTE* BY EMILY POST

Errands! I dread them. Sometimes they rule my life in a way that seems cruel and unfair. But kids need to be picked up from school, groceries need to be purchased, dry cleaning has to be dropped off. The list goes on and on. There are days when it seems all I do is run errands. But I am a mom, a wife, a living, breathing, fully functioning, multitasking adult. So I have a to-do list!

Every item on this list requires energy, and that energy begins with the look: I like to be stylistically appropriate even when I am just running errands. I hope this compulsive need of mine will translate into helping you when it's time to tackle your to-do list, keeping your life and household running as smoothly as you know it can.

First and foremost, always be prepared for the unexpected. Many of my friends and colleagues are in the public eye, so they have to pay closer attention to what they wear than the average woman. But even the average woman needs to stay on her toes in this era of cell phone cameras and Facebook. I now tell my friends, "When in doubt about your look for an errand extravaganza, ask yourself, 'If a paparazzo takes a photo of me, will I be OK with it hitting the Internet?'" If the answer is no, then redo your look. This has changed my dress for the better many, many times. And it will do the same for you.

rule breakers we love

Britney Spears

She's pulled herself together fabulously, but Ms. Spears has been known to leave the house less than fully "done." We don't necessarily want to emulate her, but she has reminded us what not to wear when buying a Slurpee (and perhaps that we should not really be buying Slurpees in the first place), and that every one of us is human and makes fashion missteps. We love her for that.

If you're a teacher, you could run into students or parents; if you're an ambitious young assistant, you might see your boss; the guy who dumped you accompanied by his modelesque new girlfriend could be in line behind you at the grocery store; the very attractive neighbor you've been trying to meet might be at the post office buying stamps just when you are; that catty woman from your spinning class could be in line at the bakery . . . I could go on and on. Have a plan. If you're often pressed for time, take a few minutes to pick out a go-to outfit to throw on when you have to run a quick errand (or six). Think: sleek, simple, functional.

You don't learn style from watching people on a runway. Fashion happens every morning when you wake up.

SHALOM HARLOW

Your go-to errand outfit can be as basic as jeans or cargo pants with a sweater and stylish sneakers. Whatever works for you, as long as it looks neat and pulled together, and you don't look like you've just emerged from a vodka bender. If you can't get your hair to cooperate, remember, that's what hats and scarves are for. Throw on a jacket or trench and, voilà, you're done.

In a pinch, a fabulous coat, sunglasses, a scarf, and boots will do the trick beautifully. You could have your Mickey Mouse pajamas on underneath that Prada overcoat. No one has to know! I always tell my friends to invest in a great coat. During the fall and winter months it's the main garment that people will see you in. Trust me, you will get great mileage out of a striking coat.

Details for Retail

What to Wear When Shopping

Nothing enlivens the spirit like a good shopping trip. Even if you don't buy anything, browsing through the racks, trying a few garments on, and admiring the gorgeous window displays can be therapeutic. It's a tactile, visual, olfactory banquet for any woman who loves fashion. And I love fashion. A serious shopping trip takes endurance and discipline; you're walking, struggling in and out of clothes, stopping for an espresso to refuel, and going back to try on that adorable cocktail dress one more time. It's delightful, and it's also a workout.

> *The quickest way to know a woman is to go shopping with her.*
>
> MARCELENE COX

Believe it or not, choosing the perfect shopping ensemble does require planning. As wonderful as this excursion may be, it's quite possible that you'll be surrounded by many, many mirrors, and a halo of hideously unflattering fluorescent lighting. These factors must be taken into account when prepping for your excursion. A woman can only be confronted by her disturbing reflection in a store's mirror a few times before fleeing to the nearest café to binge on pastry and Frappuccinos.

Don't let this happen to you. Make sure those nasty mirrors catch you on a good day, in a great outfit.

In addition to the bad lighting and cruel mirrors, another important aspect of the shopping expedition is the artificial climate of most stores—if it's cold outside, it will be an inferno inside, and vice versa. Because of an insane use of air-conditioning, the inside of a boutique in Miami can feel like an igloo in Alaska; it's bizarre. For shopping attire, layering is better than your best friend; layering is family. It allows you to effortlessly adjust to the changing temperatures of each store. Also, by layering your garments, you can preview whatever outfits you try on with a different top, sweater, or pants option, using the clothes you already own—always a plus.

You're going to think I'm crazy, but put on a little makeup. You never know if you'll end up trying on that cocktail dress you're hunting down for your best friend's engagement party. Always be comfortable, *without frumping up your look*. If you wear sloppy, you'll buy sloppy. You don't want that.

Choose adorable lingerie for your shopping trip. It doesn't have to be ultra-sexy, but you want to look your best as you slip in and out of your clothes—not for the retail assistant who is bringing you size options, and not for your friends. Wear nice things so that YOU feel gorgeous when you're buying even nicer things. Properly fitted underwear equals properly fitted outerwear.

> *I don't go out without makeup.*
> *I'm a woman, you know.*
>
> SHAKIRA

What You Should Wear

JEANS: Not super skinny or super tight jeans because, let's face it, they are not the easiest to get in and out of. Go for fitted, boot-cut jeans because they're not only manageable to get in and out of, they're incredibly versatile and go with tons of different sorts of shoes and tops.

TANK TOP OR CAMISOLE: Remember layers are key. Your underneath layer will play a pivotal role in how the tops you try on lie against your body.

COWL-NECK OR V-NECK SWEATER: I try to choose a top that won't completely muss my hair every time I take it off or put it on.

CARDIGAN: If it's cool out, I really love a long clingy cardigan with a belt. So chic.

LIGHT JACKET OR COAT: A trench looks great without overheating you during your expedition.

FLATS: Wear shoes you can walk (a lot) in, and that will look great with most of the clothes you plan to try on. Keep in mind that most boutiques have heels in various sizes, in the event you try on something that requires them. A sexy pencil skirt paired with beat-up sneakers isn't particularly flattering on anyone, but wearing heels on a shopping trip is just plain absurd.

rule breakers we love

Becky Bloomwood from *Confessions of a Shopaholic*

Our favorite shopaholic, Ms. Bloomwood, is the personification of our shopping id.

To Skirt the Issue?

You can always wear a skirt instead of jeans if that's more your style. However, wearing a dress bypasses the Layering Rule. A dress makes it a little harder to get a good idea of how separates look when you try them on, and how many different looks you can achieve using the pieces you're already wearing. As I've always said, a savvy shopper knows that whatever she buys must go with at least three things she already owns, or that item may not be worth the investment.

If you feel fabulous when you head out to shop, you will make more thoughtful purchases; you will be less tempted to buy something only to return it later. It's no big mystery—the right outfit puts you in the right mind-set.

But it's even more than that: When you go out looking great, you're saying to yourself and to the world that you will never compromise your unyielding style consistency. You are saying, "I care about myself from the inside out, at every moment of my life." Maybe it is only the cashier at your favorite department store who will really get a look at you, but hey, maybe he's cute and maybe you're single. Wink.

The most important thing a woman can have—next to talent, of course—is her hairdresser.

JOAN CRAWFORD

"Do" the Right Thing

What to Wear When You Are Getting Your Hair Done

I am a big woman. I need big hair.

ARETHA FRANKLIN

Anyone who knows me, really, really knows that I LOVE everything about hair. All the different styles that exist, the myriad of cuts, colors, lengths, and textures: silky blond tresses in perfect ponytails; sultry brunette bobs that could literally make a grown man cry; sexy soft waves with sun-kissed highlights around the face; side-swept bangs. I could go on and on. In a previous life, I'm convinced I was a hairstylist.

Whenever you go to your stylist, wear something that represents your overall personal style. Consciously or unconsciously, this initial perception of what you're wearing influences how your hair is done. This look also affects how you feel in that chair, even if you are ensconced in a giant, ugly

rule breakers we love

Lady Godiva

As the legend goes, she rode through the center of town on horseback to protest her husband's unfair tax policy with nothing but her luxurious, flowing locks covering her nudity. And that was before extensions existed!

smock. If you arrive looking sloppy or disheveled, your stylist may assume that you aren't very particular about your appearance, and in return he or she won't be very particular about your hair. We all know what happens after that. Sometimes tears, sometimes ice cream, sometimes both; never a pretty picture, regardless.

"DO" *DO'S AND DON'TS*

Rules I live by when I go in for a touch-up:

Do's

- Bring several photos of hairstyles you like. It may sound cheesy, but if you're going for a big change, come prepared to show what you want. Getting the look you desire is all about having a common point of reference with the stylist.
- Try to schedule an appointment that's NOT on the weekend. This may be impossible for some, but if you can, do it. The hustle and bustle of the weekend rush is bound to distract your stylist, no matter what he or she may tell you. Hair results are best when the salon is quiet and the artist can create in peace.
- Once your stylist is done with you, play with your hair at the salon—run your fingers through it; tousle it and brush it back into place. It's unlikely that you'll be keeping your head perfectly still after you leave the salon, right? If, after you try manipulating your coif, something's not right, you still have a last chance to correct the situation.

Don'ts

- Don't wear a shirt with a high collar, and never wear a turtleneck. This obstructs your jawline, which will alter the end effect of the cut.
- Don't watch *Tabatha's Salon Takeover* right before heading to the stylist. I love this show (she's sassy and gives great advice), but it's an anxiety-provoking behind-the-scenes look. You don't need that.
- Don't forget to tip. It's rude, and the salon will notice. You'd be surprised how quickly they will accommodate a good tipper who needs a last-minute appointment. It's not because of her winning personality.
- Don't be afraid to speak up if you question something the stylist is doing. I've held back, even though at the time I knew something was going awry. I regretted it later. Speak your mind (in a polite way); this will save you much heartache later.

Please don't misunderstand me. I'm not saying you should dress as though you are entering a beauty pageant or going on a job interview. You're not going to be subjected to a life-changing character evaluation based on this outfit. But the better you look, the more amped your stylist will be to work on you. And the more amped you will be to get a new style. Frumpiness just isn't inspiring. Be pulled together, and make sure your ensemble reflects the sort of hairstyle you want. This will make a world of difference.

> *Hair style is the final tip-off*
> *whether or not a woman really knows herself.*
>
> HUBERT DE GIVENCHY

Going Green

What to Wear When You're Gardening

Gardening is how I relax.
It's another form of creating and playing with colors.

OSCAR DE LA RENTA

I've been fascinated with growing things since I was a little girl helping my mother in her modest vegetable garden on the Caribbean coast of Colombia. We were surrounded by trees dripping with delectable tropical fruits—the mangoes were fragrant and the giant, buttery avocados were so green on the inside that they almost looked electric. My mouth waters now remembering the huge, succulent tomatoes we'd pick for our meals. And as with everything else my mother did, she knew how to garden in style.

You have to be a bit more creative to cultivate a garden in Manhattan, where I live now, but it can be done, and I encourage anyone who lives in a city to try. Start a window box or a container garden with some herbs or flowers; before you know it you'll be an organic, homegrown convert.

Gardening is one of life's simple pleasures. Nothing compares to an afternoon spent working (not too hard of course) in the sun, soaking up some nourishing vitamin D, and seeing the literal fruits of your labor blossom into vibrant, colorful life. It soothes the soul to get a little dirty, and to be one with the earth, even if it's for just a short while before returning to the realities of city life and of fashion, fashion, fashion.

rule breakers we love

Carmen Miranda

Carmen Miranda made no apologies for wearing a fruit basket on her head, and she looked damn good doing it.

Green style has come a long way since Gladys Kravitz, the nosy neighbor from *Bewitched*, in her straw hat and gardening gloves, clutched a pair of shears as she peered through the bushes at Samantha's various high jinks. Madonna recently wore a much criticized though verdant and unusual "grass"-covered Louis Vuitton dress. Madonna can do no wrong in my eyes and she certainly sent a very positive environmental message wearing that ensemble. You've got to have a sense of humor in fashion or you'll wither and die.

What You Should Wear

OVERALLS: I know I said they were a no-no before, but if there is one appropriate time for hillbilly chic, gardening is it. (Remember 1980s Brit pop sensation Dexys Midnight Runners? They were never seen without their overalls.)

BERMUDA SHORTS/CAPRI PANTS: If overalls are still too down home for you, try a classic pair of madras Bermuda shorts or capri pants in a summer print. Think Palm Beach and tall, cool highballs.

TOP: Whatever's comfortable and easy to wash. I favor a basic tee or a polo shirt when flexing my green thumb.

SHOES: Sneaks. Converse are the classic. Or, if you're irrigating, wellies.

HAT: Sun protection is no joke. Make sure to wear a sunhat with a wide, wide brim. This is not a substitute for sunblock, ladies. SPF it.

GLOVES: You've got to protect that manicure, and there are some truly sexy gardening gloves out there. Do your homework and search the Web for options you like. You can't plant a gorgeous garden without the perfect gloves.

HOW DOES YOUR GARDEN GROW?

If you want a bit of inspiration before you start planting, consider these beauties. Better yet, visit them if you can.

- LES QUATRE VENTS, QUEBEC, CANADA: Among the most acclaimed gardens in North America. They're open only four times a year, so you may have to buy the book about them by Frank Cabot if you want a look.
- JARDIN MAJORELLE, MARRAKECH, MOROCCO: This gorgeous garden, designed by the French artist Jacques Majorelle, was purchased by Yves Saint Laurent and Pierre Bergé in 1980; Yves Saint Laurent's ashes were scattered there in 2008.
- MILLENNIUM PARK, CHICAGO: The country's grandest rooftop garden.
- RYOANJI, KYOTO, JAPAN: Pure Zen serenity.
- ISOLA BELLA, ITALY: A stunning Italian mansion owned by the Borromeo family, the inspiration for the Bellagio Hotel in Las Vegas. The gardens are spectacular.
- GARDEN OF COSMIC SPECULATION, SCOTLAND: I adore the name of this place. It is a private garden owned by Charles Jencks, and it's inspired by science and math.
- BAHA'I GARDENS IN HAIFA, ISRAEL: A staircase of nineteen terraces, this magnificent labyrinthine garden is a sacred shrine of the Baha'i faith, which emphasizes unity among all cultures and religions. Flowers and peace—always a perfect combination.

I need to retire from retirement.

SANDRA DAY O'CONNOR

Only the other day I was inquiring of an entire bed of old-fashioned roses, forced to listen to my ramblings on the meaning of the universe, as I sat cross-legged in the lotus position in front of them.

PRINCE CHARLES

As if we don't have enough reasons to love our stylish first lady, Michelle Obama has started the first White House garden since the days of Eleanor Roosevelt's Victory Garden. She planted organic vegetables with the help of fifth graders from a local Washington, D.C., elementary school. And not only did these students learn to plant the vegetables, they will be returning throughout the year to harvest and cook with their very own produce.

V IS FOR VICTORY

The Victory Garden is enjoying a resurgence of popularity in the United States. During both World Wars, the government encouraged patriotic citizens to plant Victory Gardens to support the war effort, and in 1943 Americans grew nearly one-third of the nation's vegetables right in their own backyards.

rules are made to be broken

Never mix prints.

Such an old-fashioned notion. As long as you keep your prints in the same color family and don't get too crazy, go ahead and mix it up for a modern, edgy look.

So roll up your sleeves, find a plot of land (or a suitable container), get out your trowel, purchase a cornucopia of seeds, and make your garden grow. Get stylishly dirty; you know, a smudge on your nose, a rosy glow on your cheeks. Then relax with a tall glass of cold lemonade; gaze at your handiwork with satisfaction as you spend a lazy afternoon reading. *The Secret Garden* if you're feeling chaste and innocent; *My Secret Garden* if you're in a naughty mood; or *The Constant Gardener* for passionate, international adventure.

For the People

What to Wear When You're Volunteering

Volunteering feeds the soul—yours and the recipient of your beneficence. It reminds you that it's not all about you and it reinforces your obligation to the world's collective support system. Every woman should find a worthy cause to give her time and attention to. And remember, altruism and style savvy are not mutually exclusive concepts—some of the most active benefactresses are also fabulously well dressed. Princess Diana is the obvious all-star here, and Angelina Jolie is a close second. That both women have managed to look gorgeous and appropriate in the least likely circumstances is a testament to their inherent beauty, considerable flair, and, often, their publicity savvy on behalf of each worthy effort they were supporting.

So go ahead and be unabashedly stylish while putting your heart and soul into your cause. There is always a way to be fashionable without looking overdone, and looking good not only shows respect, it improves everyone's mood, including yours.

> *All I was doing was trying to get home from work.*
>
> ROSA PARKS

A woman is like a tea bag,
you cannot tell how strong she is
until you put her in hot water.

NANCY REAGAN

Soup Kitchen

Most soup kitchens can probably provide you with an apron, but there's no reason you can't bring your own fabulous apron from home. See the Holidays part on hosting Christmas or Thanksgiving for more on aprons—a recent obsession of mine.

Comfortable shoes are mandatory, since you'll probably be on your feet for quite a while. Riding boots, motorcycle boots, sneakers, or hiking boots are all good options. Soup kitchen floors can be treacherous, so pick footwear with non-skid soles. And wear what can't be ruined by spills.

Throw on jeans with a tee and layer a button-down shirt over that. You'll be able to roll up your sleeves and get down to business, and if it gets too hot and steamy, you can tie the button-down shirt around your waist.

I don't know of any way to rock a stylin' hairnet, so cross your fingers and hope you won't be asked to wear one. And just in case, bring a knit cap that can cover your coif. In rare instances, sanitation trumps style. This may be one of them.

And speaking of your coif, keep your hair pulled back off your face, and your makeup to a minimum. Plan to sweat.

Channel your inner Giada De Laurentiis. Think glowing Italian bombshell with a heart of gold.

EVERYBODY'S DOING IT

- People who volunteer are healthier and live longer than those who don't. (It's true; there's research on this.)
- Volunteering is an excellent way to meet guys. Habitat for Humanity? Men who can work with their hands? No-brainer.
- If you're considering a career change, volunteer work in a related field will provide valuable experience and look good on your résumé.
- If selflessness isn't your thing, look at volunteering as an opportunity to cultivate an air of smug altruism. I won't tell. You'll still be helping someone other than yourself. And the experience may surprise you.

I loathe narcissism, but I approve of vanity.

DIANA VREELAND

Big Brothers Big Sisters

This organization holds a special place in my heart. If you want to experience a one-on-one connection with a young person (between six and eighteen years old), this could be the volunteer opportunity for you. Helping a child muddle through adolescence into adulthood is infinitely rewarding. As you choose the perfect look for the day's activity, be aware that young minds are impressionable and parents can be protective of their children, so dress modestly. It doesn't hurt to sport some Rocawear or Adidas; but just enough to look like you're in touch with youthful fashion, not its victim.

VOLUNTEERS WE LOVE

- JERRY LEWIS, Telethon for Muscular Dystrophy: Say what you will about his movies (they make me laugh), Jerry Lewis has been a dedicated fundraiser for MDA (Muscular Dystrophy Association) every year since 1955.
- QUINCY JONES, MICHAEL JACKSON, AND LIONEL RICHIE, USA for Africa: "We Are the World" was one of the best-selling pop singles ever, and it raised over $63 million for humanitarian aid in the United States and Africa. Lionel Richie and Quincy Jones had already planned to record a new version of the song for its twenty-fifth anniversary before the 2010 earthquake in Haiti. The new incarnation of "We Are the World" has raised even more money for the victims of that tragedy.
- ELIZABETH TAYLOR, HIV/AIDS: Liz deserves some props for being one of the first celebrities to speak out publicly for HIV/AIDS awareness.
- BILL AND MELINDA GATES, Bill & Melinda Gates Foundation: Dedicated to promoting healthy, productive lives in developing countries, and success at school and life in under-resourced parts of the United States. Not only has Bill Gates helped to make "geeks" cool, he's made charitable foundations even cooler.
- YASMIN AGA KHAN, the daughter of Prince Aly Khan of Pakistan and the exquisite Rita Hayworth, was deeply influenced by the passing of her mother from Alzheimer's disease. Her philanthropic efforts in raising awareness of the effects of the disease have touched millions.

ASPCA

A basket of puppies may be the ultimate mood elevator. But be forewarned, volunteering at the ASPCA (the American Society for the Prevention of Cruelty to Animals) is not for the faint of heart. I can't sugarcoat this: You're going to be dealing with a lot of drool and poop, so wear jeans or cargo pants, sturdy old shoes you're not afraid of ruining, and long sleeves (those kitties have sharp claws). Don't wear white and do wear clothes you aren't very attached to.

Think urban rancher or sexy zookeeper. Even better, picture Jennifer Lopez as an adorable and sporty dogwalker in *Monster-in-Law*.

Habitat for Humanity

Building a house is fabulous exercise for the spirit and the body. The entire experience is a workout! And hey, you never know, you could wind up learning a trade. Besides, knowing how to drywall and install plumbing makes any girl quite the catch.

Wear work clothes. Steel-toe boots are preferable, or anything with a sturdy outer shell to them, as you never know what heavy object may fall onto your feet. Trucker hats are still in if you're painting or doing carpentry, so dig your nineties relic out of the closet and go for it.

Think practical grunge. Pull out your plaid shirts and oh so retro dungarees.

The Avon Walk for Breast Cancer or Susan G. Komen Race for the Cure

Great exercise for a great cause. Unfortunately, odds are that you've been affected by breast cancer through someone you know and love. Fortunately, you can have fun *and* make a difference.

Good walking or running shoes are essential. You must protect your joints and feet while working out for this cause. You don't want anything to prevent you from wearing your stilettos later, do you? Take care of those feet!

The color pink springs to mind when I envision my Breast Cancer Awareness ensemble. Sport a pink wristband. And work the pink any other way you can. No color speaks as forcefully for the collective cause of femininity.

You'll probably get a T-shirt with an inspirational message to wear for the walk. Being a woman who doesn't wear athletic tees in my daily life, I bring a small pair of scissors and a few safety pins to make fashionable on-the-spot alterations.

Think *Flashdance* chic. You can't go wrong with Under Armour.

Style Sessions

What to Wear to Therapy

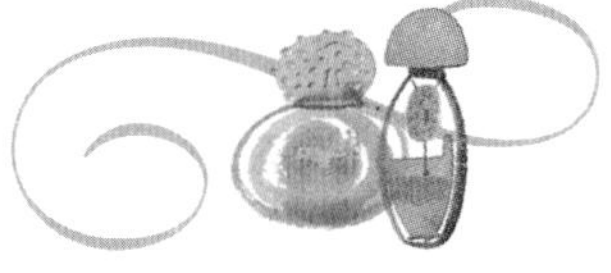

A particularly beautiful woman is a source of terror.

CARL JUNG

I realize that many women don't even like to mention whether or not they see a therapist, much less discuss how to dress for the occasion; but this is precisely why so many don't know what to wear! It's actually an interesting style situation. One could easily argue that whatever you wear is in some way a subconscious reflection of your current psychological state. Your clothes are the first thing people see about you; your willingness to don them undoubtedly says something about how you are feeling at any given moment. I'm going to hazard a guess that many therapists are not especially attuned to the subtleties of fashion. Well, they should be.

A very good friend of mine was seeing a therapist whose fashion sense truly perplexed and disturbed her. As soon as her appointment ended she would call me with the latest visual atrocity her shrink had dared to showcase.

"Oh my god, she was wearing hooker boots and a hideous blue jacket with shoulder pads! I don't even remember what we talked about; I spent the entire time trying to figure out what made her put that outfit on today."

Or, "Why a beret? Why would she wear a beret at a rakish angle while she's seeing patients? I just might need therapy to work through my therapy."

Ultimately my friend was so distracted by her therapist's attire that

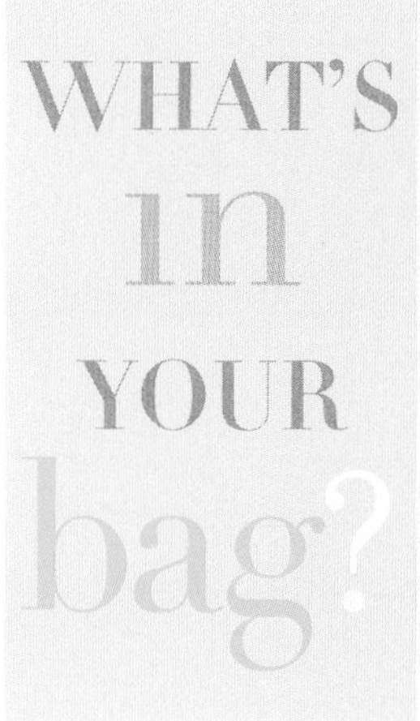

There are way too many jokes to be made about baggage and therapy, so I will just say, "What type of bag do *you* think you need?" Bring something easy to carry and simple. Be sure to include tissues and a touch-up kit. A little spritz of fragrance will do wonders to revitalize your spirit after a taxing session about your life.

she began to question her doctor's judgment and decided to stop seeing her altogether. Conversely, while I know (or pray) none of you are wearing hooker boots and a beret anywhere (much less to work!), my friend's experience can serve to remind you of the importance of personal style in this intimate setting.

As always, my mantra is wear whatever makes you feel fabulous, but do make sure you feel comfortable and at ease in whatever you wear to therapy. Be yourself. Therapy is a healing place. Simply by entering that room and sitting on that couch or chair, you've made a step toward bettering your life; but remember that from the moment you've walked into that room, even before you've begun to speak, you're communicating. Don't muddle up the moment with a strong print or outlandish heels that will distract your therapist. This is serious work. Take a pashmina with you, so you can wrap yourself with something warm and cozy, always reassuring when you're just about to bare your soul.

> *When you ask people about their clothes, what they do is tell you about their lives.*
>
> DELIA EPHRON

Over Easy

What to Wear for Brunch with the Girls

She generally gave herself very good advice (though she seldom followed it).

FROM *ALICE'S ADVENTURES IN WONDERLAND* BY LEWIS CARROLL

Sunday brunch is one of my very favorite social customs—a luxury I can't indulge in nearly as often as I'd like. The aroma of freshly brewed coffee in the air, adorable couples with perfectly mussed hair reading their Sunday papers, plates of delicious comfort food parading in and out of the kitchen, bacon slabs still sizzling when they reach the table. From our earliest years together in New York, my friends and I have been getting together to nurse hangovers, give (and get) copious amounts of advice, replay the highlights from the night before, and gossip with abandon. And those conversations are even more interesting over eggs and champagne. By now we've replaced most of our boy talk and hangover recovery rhetoric with childcare talk and career advice, but the pleasures of our gossip, our friendships, and the delicious food will endure forever.

> *It's the friends you can call up at 4 A.M. that matter.*
>
> MARLENE DIETRICH

Brunch wear seems like a no-brainer, right? After all, it's your BFFs or family. They don't care what you have on; they've seen you through your lowest moments. They brought you tissues and ice cream when you were nursing a broken heart; they know what you look like when you've cried so much your eyes have swollen shut. And anyway, it's Sunday—the one day of the week that you can take a break from looking fabulous.

Wrong.

Yes, your nearest and dearest love you for you—not how you look—but let's face it; unconscious wardrobe inventory is an involuntary reflex for most of us. We all sneak in the "up-and-down" glance and check off (whether we admit it or not) our internal list: *She's working it*, or *She put a serious dent in her credit card this week*, or *She's wearing the exact same thing she wore last Sunday*, or *What's with the roots?*, and on and on. Almost simultaneously, as you're filing away these tidbits about your friends, the inevitable internal backlash about you begins to set in: *Oh my god, did I wear THIS last Sunday? Do I look fat in these pants? Is that toothpaste on my shirt?*

So, while brunch doesn't require the level of attention to detail that you give a first date outfit, it does merit consideration.

First, Ask Yourself These Questions

Do I look fabulous? Always look fabulous.
Am I comfortable? It's brunch; you'll need a little room in your waistband.
Am I overdressed? You don't want to seem as though you're trying to outshine anyone—they're your friends, but they're also women, and social harmony is a must.

What You Should Wear

DRESS: This is *the* time for a billowy maxi dress in a gorgeous floral print, with a pretty pair of ballet flats and a chic scarf. You're ready to go in an instant and you'll have plenty of room for post-brunch expansion. If it's really chilly outside, just throw on some tights and that perfect vintage motorcycle jacket.

PANTS: A great pair of boyfriend jeans or paper bag pants; they're comfy-chic.

SHIRT: A fitted tee or tailored shirt—never go with a too baggy top and bottom. Also keep in mind we *don't* want to see four inches of cleavage before noon. A classic Breton tee or anything by Michael Stars or American Apparel always looks lovely.

JACKET: A luxurious cardigan or a great blazer.

SHOES: You don't need to pull out the stilettos for a casual brunch. Wear shoes you can walk in. Chances are you'll want to take a stroll or do some shopping after all that girl talk. Slouchy boots are my personal favorite, or car shoes.

ACCESSORIES: Always, always, always remember your shades! The bigger the better to hide last night's excesses.

rule breakers we love

Gwen Stefani

A true mix master when it comes to blending plaids and stripes, or bright blue hair with a fuzzy blue bra, Gwen Stefani always looks as though she'd be the perfect woman to sit with and recap the weekend's festivities.

Spring and fall are the best seasons for brunching. Food always tastes better when you eat outside, and a good dose of sunshine nourishes the spirit like nothing else, but even when it's cold and gray, you can embody the al fresco spirit with a cheerful splash of color. Add an unusual accessory such as a vintage brooch, a chunky necklace, or some funky shoes. A little flair is a great conversation starter—there's nothing like an assemblage of pretty objects at the table for women to look at while they chat.

And don't forget the weather report. A stylish woman must always consider the weather.

Obviously, when getting ready to brunch it up, one's personal style must be taken into account just as it is on any other occasion. And a woman who is into studs and leather will not suddenly go the way of cashmere and turtlenecks (though she really should try to ease up on the hardware on Sunday morning).

THE BEST OF BRUNCH

MOST POPULAR BRUNCH FOOD: Eggs Benedict

BEST BRUNCH COCKTAILS: Bloody Mary or Bellini

THE PERFECT BLOODY MARY: 2 ounces of vodka (I like Grey Goose); a dash of red wine; a pinch of celery salt, pepper, and salt; 7 drops of Worcestershire sauce; 5 drops of hot sauce; 6 ounces of tomato juice; and a celery stalk

BEST BRUNCH ALTERNATIVE: Dim Sum

BEST BRUNCH HANGOVER CURE: This is not the time to stick to your diet: Load up on carbs and grease, and drink plenty of water.

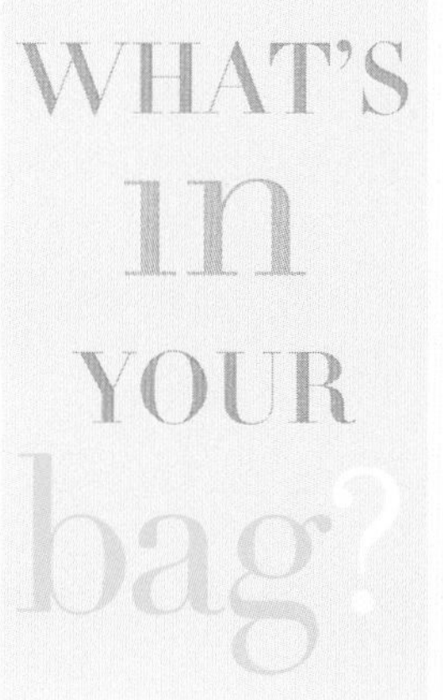

WHAT'S in YOUR bag?

The tote is the perfect brunch bag. You'll want plenty of room for the Sunday *Times*, and the baguette and bottle of wine you'll pick up on your way home.

When you can't eat another bite and you're running out of conversation (it happens), spend a lazy afternoon in the park people-watching. Or go window-shopping to round out the full experience. Going to a late afternoon movie is also an excellent way to maximize a relaxing Sunday that will help refuel you for another long week ahead.

Pearl necklaces and jewels in the mornings are monstrous, no matter what the fashion of the moment may decree.

FROM *ETIQUETTE FOR AMERICANS*, BY A WOMAN OF FASHION, 1898

night

Enchanté

What to Wear to a Cocktail Party

Something about glamour interested me. All of my schoolbooks had drawings of women on terraces with a cocktail and a cigarette.

BILL BLASS

I can almost hear the ice clinking in the glasses right now. It's a good thing I love a cocktail party; in my business I sometimes attend a cocktail party or two every night of the week. So believe me when I tell you that I have this down to a science. Cocktail parties are about elegant, showstopping outfits that turn heads. Period, the end.

A cocktail dress *is* the obvious wardrobe choice. But exactly what is a cocktail dress? The definition is fairly broad: In years past, it was a semiformal frock with a hem falling anywhere from just above the knee to just above the ankle; these days the hem can be as high as you dare, and on weekend nights at the beach, a floor-length maxi dress is divine.

Take this opportunity to indulge in luxurious fabrics and a bit of exotic embellishment. Ruffles, feathers, beading, or sequins are all welcome at a cocktail party—though, generally, not all on one dress. Silk jersey, velvet, brocade, chiffon, tulle—the sky is the limit when it comes to fabric. Of course cotton and denim are always options (I'm not sure anyone can make terry cloth work for a cocktail party, though I never say never), but why not take advantage of the opportunity to be slightly more glamorous than you are every day?

SEQUINS 101: WHAT TO LOOK FOR

- When shopping for the sequined party frock that makes everyone in the room stop and say, "Who's that girl?," quality is key. Don't go overboard or you can end up looking like a has-been Broadway diva.
- Size matters: If the sequins are too big they can get costumey.
- Lining: A lining makes any garment look better and this is even truer with sequins. It keeps threads from catching on your undergarments and it ensures your clothing will hold its shape under the weight of its glitz.
- Matte sequins are modern and low-key.
- Jet beading is subtle and adds elegant luster.
- Stick to a single color. Multicolored sequins can be a bit overwhelming.

Evening is a time of real experimentation. You never want to look the same way.

DONNA KARAN

Pretty and glamorous are the rule when preparing for a cocktail party, so your hair and makeup should be just that. Think Anne Bancroft's highlights in *The Graduate*.

Glamour is the power to rearrange people's emotions, which, in effect, is the power to control one's environment.

ARTHUR MILLER

What You Should Wear

SEPARATES: Silky pants and a sequined tunic are an excellent alternative to the cocktail dress. You can also wear sequined baggy peg leg trousers (very YSL), a silk jumpsuit, or sharp tuxedo pants. And yes, it's official, shorts are appropriate for evening as long as you are in a tropical climate and the shorts are in a luxe fabric, such as silk, and paired with great shoes. Shorts with opaque tights and stilettos make your legs look extra long and lean. Add a silk blouse, throw on a tuxedo jacket, and you're ready for action.

A COCKTAIL DRESS: When I'm in a hurry, nothing is easier than the trusty LBD (little black dress). It's easy to accessorize, always slimming, total perfection. Black does not have to be boring; mixing textures or matte and shiny materials adds an interesting edge to your basic black—perhaps a patent leather belt or shoes, or a satin jacket over a crepe dress. For a posh event, I wear something simple and elegant. A tailored silhouette with a skirt that hits just below the knee is becoming to almost every figure. Anything that falls more than an inch or two below the knee to just above the ankle is a tough length to pull off, unless the skirt is very, very fitted or you are Grace Jones. Believe me.

If I'm attending a fashion industry soiree, I go for an edgier look: asymmetry, strong color, and sophistication. To a more laid-back, no-fuss party, opt for pretty, low-key chic. Semiformal attire allows for some playfulness and color, so break out of your chromatic rut and try a gorgeous jewel tone or a rich, deep red or burnt orange.

WRAP: "Wrap" sounds even more luxurious than jacket or coat; it is so much more tactile. Wear one that sets off your dress to perfection. A sequin-encrusted number will encase you in a cloud of sparkle. In cold weather, choose a sumptuous velvet wrap, or a sensuous faux fur chubby, stole, vest, or bolero. Watch *Bus Stop* with Marilyn Monroe for the comical, sexy, and drawn-out scene where she's being helped into (or out of) her coat. She knows how to appreciate a wrap. Her corsets in this film are also to die for.

SHOES: Strappy heels are spectacular with cocktail attire. Metallics add glam to a simple dress. And booties? They're modern and chic—especially with pretty lace or pattern stockings to add a little texture and whimsy. Invest in a good pair of heels; you've got to be ready to mix and mingle, and the cocktail party is the quintessential moment for height and presence. Channel an ancient goddess on her pedestal.

ACCESSORIES: This is the moment when you can have fun with all of your bijouterie. A little black dress is the perfect backdrop for a statement piece. Stunning drop earrings with an updo, an ornate cuff, or bangles to show off a toned arm. Always make sure your jewelry isn't taking over you or your ensemble and keep everything in proportion to your frame. Don't weigh down your dainty wrist with a heavy cuff and don't let your athletic physique dwarf your delicate bangles. Balance is key in dressing and in life.

BAG: A clutch or small bag is another accessory, so choose wisely. A vintage bag is always a lovely accent piece. Other alternatives are a clutch bag made of soft material like leather, satin, or mesh; a box clutch, which is harder and usually geometric; or a jeweled minaudière.

rule breakers we love

Jeanne Moreau

Jeanne Moreau's smoldering beauty and glamorous style have made her irresistible to directors and audiences alike. She's a femme fatale in every sense—a thinking man's Brigitte Bardot. Watch *Jules and Jim*, *Viva Maria*, *The Bride Wore Black*, or any of her numerous films to see her magnetism in action.

rules are made to be broken

Your bag must match your shoes perfectly.

Of course your bag shouldn't *clash* with your shoes (or anything else you have on), but the notion that you need a different evening bag for every pair of heels you might wear is rather old-fashioned. Choose a bag that complements your ensemble. For instance, if you're wearing black with a patterned or brightly colored shoe, go for something like a black beaded clutch with a detail or trim that picks up a color from the shoe.

SET THE MOOD

- Listen to some classic jazz such as Art Blakey, Duke Ellington, or Esquivel for that sixties party flair.
- Watch *Breakfast at Tiffany's*, *Sabrina*, *The Party*, *La Dolce Vita*. Total glam.
- Match your nail polish to your lipstick. And definitely make sure the polish isn't chipped.
- Bone up on current events. You want lots of material for small talk.
- Buy fresh flowers for the host.
- Have one glass of water for every alcoholic beverage you consume, to keep you hydrated and scare away tomorrow's hangover.

As a rule, a cocktail party is a pre-dinner affair. However, it can also take place after the dinner hour or even instead of dinner. Heavy appetizers will probably be served on such occasions; no one wants unhappy guests. Luckily, the invite should provide you with all of the relevant information about a start and end time, as well as the dress code.

A lady shouldn't spend the evening grazing on appetizers, so have a snack before you head out to curb your craving for the banquet of bite-size delicacies. This is a must for me because I LOVE hors d'oeuvres and it's far too easy to overindulge without even realizing you've just consumed an entire tray of canapés.

These fetes are made for socializing, networking, and having a good time admiring how fabulous everyone looks. Holly Golightly's sensational soiree in *Breakfast at Tiffany's* epitomizes the anything-goes combined with old-school-chic vibe of the perfect cocktail party. This is your moment to revel and relish in the complete joy that comes with being a woman—a world of total creativity where style and femininity are the ingredients to play with. The cocktail party allows us to feature our best accessories and our favorite fragrances; and it gives us a reason to get our hair done and spend an extra ten minutes on our triceps at the gym. So blot your lipstick, powder your nose, and go have a great time.

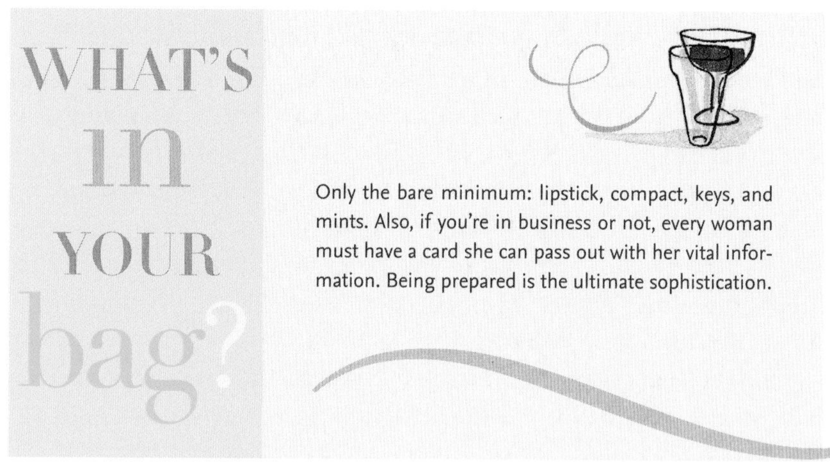

WHAT'S in YOUR bag?

Only the bare minimum: lipstick, compact, keys, and mints. Also, if you're in business or not, every woman must have a card she can pass out with her vital information. Being prepared is the ultimate sophistication.

Bon Appétit, My Sweet

What to Wear to a Black-Tie Dinner

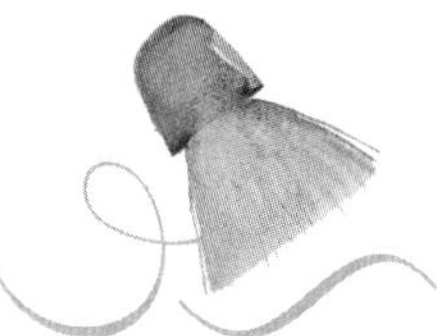

Serve the dinner backward, do anything—but for goodness sake, do something weird.

ELSA MAXWELL

It's such fun getting dressed for a full-on, formal dinner. For starters, it means I won't be tottering around in heels all night—but instead ensconced in comfort, enjoying delicious food and good company. Wine will pour, the laughs will get louder, and there very well may be Alka-Seltzer at the end of the story. What joy. But seriously, formality is a dying art in this hectic world we live in; it's enchanting and refreshing to embody grace and propriety now and then. When I'm totally decked out, I'm instantly transported to when I was a little girl playing dress-up in my mother's closet, emulating the glamour she exuded as guests began to arrive for one of the fabulous dinners she was known for. I tap into that feeling as often as I can.

Traditionally a formal dinner dress is a sleeveless, floor-length gown with gorgeous décolletage. The key difference between a dinner dress and a ball gown is that the ball gown has a full skirt, while the dinner dress can have either a full or a fitted skirt. That's all in the past.

Today, it's completely appropriate to wear a shorter dress or even pants. Take full advantage of a formal dinner, where you can practice the fine art of a structured, glamorous look (and wear your best heels!).

I can get a better grasp of what is going on in the world from one good Washington dinner party than from all the background information piled on my desk.

BARBARA WALTERS

What You Should Wear

DRESS: Floor length, in a luxurious fabric. Nothing compares to beautiful draping; a Grecian goddess style looks fabulous on almost every body type, and you can sit and eat without worrying about the seams. Or go for something along the lines of the stunningly simple sheath. When in doubt, think Audrey Hepburn in *Breakfast at Tiffany's* or Rita Hayworth in *Gilda*. A touch of architectural pleating, asymmetry, or vibrant color will give your classic glamour a contemporary finish.

SKIRT: Separates are always a welcome, and a slightly more versatile, alternative. A gorgeous long bias-cut skirt with a great top that has some beading, sequins, or other embellishment is perfectly chic—but only if you are tall and willowy, or plan to wear your highest platforms. Other options are a full skirt with a cinched waist or a modern bustle skirt in raw silk or satin. Both are easy to wear and look spectacular.

TOP: Go for crisp and tailored, a fitted, embellished shell, or anything with flair that makes you feel dressed up. Strapless, camisole, halter, you name it. The only thing more dazzling than diamonds at cocktail parties are shoulders, so show them off. A formal dinner isn't the place for a plunging neckline, so why not try a low back? Not too low, mind you, just enough for a tasteful entrance.

WRAP: Depending on the temperature, you can wear a glittery scarf or a short faux fur bolero. Or try a sequin, brocade, or tuxedo jacket. If it's very cold, wear a warm coat over all, and stow it the moment you arrive. Burberry Prorsum and Elizabeth & James have tons of terrific coats.

SHOES: Heels, the higher and strappier, the better. If you can't deal with stilettos, satin ballet flats will work too. But heels belong at dinner parties.

ACCESSORIES: You can bring out your best jewelry for a distinguished affair. A metallic or Swarovski embellished belt, for example, or the famed cocktail ring. Gloves also give a playful nod to traditional evening dress. Take this occasion to showcase a statement necklace or bold earrings—but pick one or the other. Restraint is key!

Formal dinner dress implies a certain austerity, but formal wear should never be stiff or stodgy. Your best accessory is an air of ease and confidence.

rule breakers we love

Michelle Obama

Our first lady's audacious style has us all mesmerized. She blends high and low fashion beautifully, embraces color, and isn't afraid to take risks—from J.Crew sweaters to the black and red Narciso Rodriguez dress she wore on election night, to the lemongrass Isabel Toledo sheath and coat she wore on Inauguration Day, to the deceptively simple Jason Wu gown she wore for the Inaugural Ball. She embraces her statuesque, athletic physique, and always remains true to her personal style.

DRESS CODE 101: DECODING THE PARTY INVITATION

- CASUAL: Whatever you want, within reason of course; it's still a party. Don't wear your cargo pants, and if you are going to wear jeans, dress them up with something snazzy on top.
- BUSINESS CASUAL: Office attire.
- FESTIVE: Think cocktail with a tad more whimsy and glitter.
- COCKTAIL: This calls for your LBD or other equally fabulous party dress.
- BUSINESS FORMAL: Basically semiformal, but err on the prim side.
- SEMIFORMAL/INFORMAL: See Cocktail.
- FORMAL: Wear an evening gown or very dressy separates.
- BLACK-TIE OPTIONAL: As the name implies, slightly less formal than black tie.
- BLACK TIE: For women, black tie equals formal; for men it means wear a tux.
- WHITE TIE: The most formal of formal wear is required. Men must wear a white tie, with vest, and the whole nine yards. Women are expected to wear evening gowns.

Take your time preparing for a formal dinner party. Get a massage in the afternoon and listen to music while you primp. Don't leave getting ready until the last minute; you want to avoid catastrophes such as walking into a cocktail party with a head of wet hair or speeding through your makeup so fast that you end up looking more like a harlequin than Jean Harlow—it's far better to be fashionably late than unfashionably groomed. Take your time, enjoy the process; you are a princess for the evening. Savor it.

THE coif THE face

An updo shows off your gorgeous neck and shoulders. If you have shorter hair, keep it smooth and off your face. Katherine Heigl and Charlize Theron have both worn showstopping chin-length coifs on the red carpet. Charlize often wears minimal, glowing, tawny makeup, and Katherine favors simple eyes, rosy cheeks, and red, red lips. Watch and learn from them.

Curtains Up

What to Wear to a Broadway Play

The theatre is a spiritual and social X-ray of its time.

STELLA ADLER

Ah, live theater: the orchestra tuning up, the crowd pouring slowly into the room, the audience's whispers and comments of eager anticipation, the ushers guiding each ticket holder to her seat as if there were no more important task on the planet. The whole experience is simply divine.

You will need an outfit worthy of the thrill and grandeur of the theater, an ensemble that transforms you into one of the glitterati, attracting admiration before, during, and after intermission. Make the most of your night; arrange to have early cocktails and a late supper. Americans so rarely see live performances anymore—make an event out of it.

Going Broadway

As you know, I revel in putting together an outfit that reflects the mood of the occasion. For a night out at the theater, I love to play with the notion of costume and theatrics by paying homage to the evening's show through my own wardrobe. Subtlety is key here; I'm not suggesting you arrive looking like Daisy Mae in *Li'l Abner*, or worse, Little Orphan Annie. Just an homage. For instance, to see *Chicago*, accessorize with an extra-long strand of vintage glass beads from the twenties or a pair of gorgeous Prada Mary Janes—they have that bygone-era-meets-today's-woman timelessness of all things Prada. Everything else should be thoroughly modern. It makes an evening extra special when you can have a little fun with a style theme or motif.

rule breakers we love

Sally Bowles

The most memorable femme fatale in musical theater. Liza Minnelli's film interpretation of Ms. Bowles in *Cabaret* is iconic. She was the perfect blend of heavy, sooty eyes with lashes for days, scarlet lips, and beauty mark in place—equal parts showgirl, prostitute, and tragic heroine. Her sequined halter romper with fishnets and top hat was unforgettable. Sally Bowles put on a brave, devil-may-care face no matter what her circumstances, and she did it with flourish.

What You Should Wear

DRESS: Something fun and a tad grandiose such as a black sheath with some beaded embellishment or trim inspired by Louis Vuitton or Lanvin. (Their clothes are wonderfully extravagant.) Think striking color, panache, and flair.

WRAP: A luxe opera coat or a short faux fur jacket.

SHOES: Glamorous goddess platforms. Brian Atwood comes to mind.

ACCESSORIES: Sparkle! Wear statement earrings or a cocktail ring, or both.

When dressing for dramatic effect, do something unexpected. Don't be afraid to mix things up by pairing a military style jacket with a velvet skirt, vintage with modern, off the rack with couture, formal with casual. If you wear all black, add striking color with shoes or a bib necklace. Try to create an unusual silhouette with high-waisted narrow trousers and a blousy top or blousy trousers with a fitted top and a bolero. As always, work with your figure; draping, pleats, and proportion can work miracles when it comes to hiding flaws and enhancing assets.

I'm going to go out on a limb here and say that my favorite Broadway production of all time was *Cabaret* at the old Studio 54. Café tables replaced traditional theater seating, Natasha Richardson was sublime as Sally Bowles, and costume designer William Ivey Long's use of vintage was superb. (If you ever needed lingerie inspiration, this was the show to see.) The audience was enveloped in the ambiance of the music, the drama, and the amazing location.

THE coif THE face

Overall look? Dramatic elegance.

Sweep your hair into a tousled bun or leave it down in soft, sexy waves. If you have short, chin-length hair, this is a great time to work the bob, so get out the gel and make sure there's not a hair out of place. And experiment with your makeup. Try a dramatic, smoky eye and pale lips; or clean, graphic liquid liner and scarlet lips with a slight opalescent sheen.

Air kiss, and off you go.

THEATRICS WITHOUT THE THEATER

If you can't go to the theater, these diversions can make you feel as if you did.

- *Chicago*: Watch Renee Zellweger, Queen Latifah, and Catherine Zeta-Jones in this Oscar-winning film. Zeta-Jones's showstopping performance of "All That Jazz" makes me want to throw on a pair of fishnets and kick up my legs.
- *The Lion King*: Book an African safari—a photo safari of course—then you can get a close-up of the real thing. If that's a bit too much for you, just watch a documentary and listen to the soundtrack of the musical.
- *Cabaret*: Find a great karaoke bar and belt out your best version of "Wilkommen."
- *Mamma Mia!*: That's easy, just throw some ABBA on your iPod and rock out.
- *Rent*: Bundle up in a striped wool scarf, brew a good cup of coffee, and listen to "La Vie Bohème."
- *Angels in America*: Mike Nichols directed this Golden Globe and Emmy Award–winning HBO miniseries about the scourge of AIDS, and of bigotry, in six fascinating episodes. Settle in with a box of tissues and get ready to cry.

I think of life itself now as a wonderful play that I've written for myself, and so my purpose is to have the utmost fun playing my part.

SHIRLEY MACLAINE

The Gallery Crawl

What to Wear to an Art Opening

I've never believed in God, but I believe in Picasso.

DIEGO RIVERA

An art opening is an excellent occasion for people-watching and mingling. It's a blend of street scene, art scene, business, and glamour, all in one place. Everyone is eager to see and be seen. I generally don't even try to get a close look at the art at an opening; I save that experience for a later visit to the gallery. However, the "art" factor does open up the door to stylistic whimsy. Play with your look; push your sartorial envelope—this does not mean you should wear a dress in the shape of a swan (Björk). The opening party is about congratulating the artist *and* socializing. You'll want to flex your style muscles here, without compromising your sense of balance.

After saying my hellos, I like to stand off to the side for a moment and just take it all in; the myriad of people and styles circulating throughout the space. You see it all: from Swarovski crystals, sequins, and buttery leather to neon-colored lace, peacock feathers, and shredded jeans. And rest assured, everyone else is also rapt in people-watching delight. The party is almost like an art installation in and of itself.

Anything becomes interesting if you look at it long enough.

GUSTAVE FLAUBERT

As a rule, gallery openings are less formal than museum openings, but both can run the gamut. Before choosing an outfit consider these questions: Is it uptown (translation "elegant") or downtown (translation "edgy")? Is it an opening for an emerging artist or an established one? Is it invitation only or open to the public? Emerging artists' parties attract the most interesting crowds—eclectic, bohemian, hipster extravaganzas that are unbelievably inspiring; many high-fashion looks are born here, in the style trenches. Attend as many of these as possible.

If you are dressing for a gallery opening after work, your wardrobe options will be somewhat limited. Never fear, it's always possible to style it up if you plan ahead. Wear your basic office look—a pencil skirt or skinny trousers, a blazer, and pumps. Put on a graphic tee under your buttoned-up professional blazer and wear a pair of patterned tights. Before you go out, switch the blazer for a killer leather jacket and replace your pumps with edgy booties, or tuck your pants into a pair of thigh-high boots. You'll instantly be downtown ready.

rule breakers we love

Daphne Guinness

Muse, heiress, and all around Renaissance woman Daphne Guinness personifies the marriage of art and fashion. She marches to the beat of her own drum. Daphne's clothing is her art; she and Lady Gaga are probably the only two women in the world who can wear Alexander McQueen's twelve-inch heels without looking ridiculous.

For an uptown affair, you're practically ready to go from work just as you are. Add a little sparkle with a cocktail ring or a bib necklace. Make your cheeks glow with a dash of blush. Freshen up with a spritz of fragrance, a touch of scarlet lipstick, and you're off.

Cities and towns that aren't art world meccas like New York, L.A., or Chicago have begun to celebrate their visionaries—local art galleries and artists—with regular Art Walks or First Friday events. On these occasions, you can stroll from exhibit to exhibit, appreciating the local talent and the other art aficionados. Why not make a night of it and take the time to do it up?

When you are well dressed and fierce, it's life enhancing for you and all the people around you.

SIMON DOONAN

What You Should Wear

SKIRT: The key word is playful. Wear an unusual cut or color, or an innovative fabric. Go for asymmetrical, volume, fringe, mini, faux fur, shiny, or glitzy. Whatever strikes your fancy as long as it's close to the cutting edge.

TROUSERS: See above. Or throw on some ultrahip denim; there are endless variations on the traditional jean. Check out J Brand or Current/Elliott.

BLOUSE: Try a graphic tee or an embellished blouse. Ruffles or shoulder pads (not both at once; the goal is avant-garde, not circus clown) or interesting cutouts.

JACKET: Edgy leather, faux fur, or an innovative shape. Whatever you wear, own your look.

SHOES: Platforms are fabulous for openings because they're gorgeous and comfortable and they give you added height, putting you head and shoulders above the crowd.

HOSIERY: A must if you want to enliven your overall look. Black is always an option and fantastic, colorful hosiery is an ideal way to spice it up—and show off your gorgeous legs.
ACCESSORIES: Think wearable art but beware of wearable arts and crafts. Take this opportunity to make a statement with your jewelry; an unusual piece is eye-catching and a great conversation starter.
BAG: Wear something that won't obscure your outfit or the view. A modest shoulder bag or clutch will move through the crowd with ease.

THE coif THE face

Anything goes when it comes to your hair. If you ever thought about trying a new style, an art opening is the place to do it. An art opening is also an ideal time for a dusting of glitter on your cheekbones, and the modified cat eye or heavy liner (just make sure you use some dark shadow in the crease of the eyelid, to avoid the Amy Winehouse look). A nude lip gloss will complement your glamorous eyes. Ready? Shoulders back, head up, and stride confidently into the gallery or museum, as if you own the place.

ARTFUL COLLABORATIONS

- ELSA SCHIAPARELLI AND SALVADOR DALÍ: The two collaborated on several dresses throughout her career, including the famous 1937 "Lobster Dress," a simple, white evening dress with a large drawing of a lobster, by Dalí, on the skirt.
- TAKASHI MURAKAMI AND LOUIS VUITTON: In 2002 artist Takashi Murakami's groundbreaking collaboration with Louis Vuitton not only created playfully colored handbags, but opened the floodgates to a multitude of creative partnerships between Murakami and Vuitton.
- GAP AND VARIOUS FINE ARTISTS: In 2002 Gap introduced a line of Artist Edition Tees designed by talents such as Jeff Koons, Kenny Scharf, Barbara Kruger, Chuck Close, and Kiki Smith.
- STELLA MCCARTNEY AND JEFF KOONS: In 2006 Stella McCartney debuted Chrome Bunny bracelets and print dresses inspired by pop art bad boy Jeff Koons.
- ZAHA HADID AND CHANEL: In 2008 architect Zaha Hadid designed a mobile museum to house a traveling exhibition of art pieces inspired by the classic quilted Chanel handbag.
- AZARRO AND KUNTZEL + DEYGAS: In 2009 Azarro, guided by Vanessa Seward, worked with the French artists on a limited edition consisting of two scarves, denim trench coats and bags, and a bottle of Azzaro Couture perfume with images of their characters "The Doll and the Bear."
- ANYA HINDMARCH AND BEN EINE: In 2010 Anya Hindmarch collaborated on a line of totes with images by London street artist Ben Eine.

Bordeaux Baby

What to Wear to a Wine Tasting

A wine tasting is a banquet for the senses. And there is something almost spiritual about it, as if the ceremony of tasting actually reconnects you to the earth and its glorious cycles. If I were stranded on a desert island with just wine, cheese, and some fresh fruit, I'd be a very, very content woman.

For now, though, picture yourself on a veranda overlooking the ocean. The sky is a crystalline azure, a breeze is blowing the scent of salt water, and waves are crashing in the background. Or picture yourself après an afternoon of exploring vineyards, relaxing with a glass of Bordeaux so pretty you almost want to give it a girl's name.

You will be wearing something comfortable, chic, and worthy of vinification's long history and lore.

Wine is constant proof that
God loves us and loves to see us happy.

BENJAMIN FRANKLIN

HAUTE DRINKING

In 1976, a group of French wine experts held a blind tasting in Paris. Much to their horror, two Napa Valley vintages beat out the French wines in their category. It was a global scandal in the world of wine. Wine has taken the United States by storm ever since.

I can't think of a better excuse for socializing, indulging in a few tapas, and lounging about looking fabulous than a wine-tasting event. I recently attended a lovely wine tasting thrown by a friend. She invited each of the guests to bring a bottle or two of their favorite vintage, and she displayed the bottles on a buffet along with delicious little snacks. The diversity of the wines was thrilling, and the party gave everyone a chance to express their individual taste. Conviviality and cultural education are always a great match.

What You Should Wear

SEPARATES: Think eighties Armani. Simple tunics and wide-legged pants in light fabrics like silk jersey or diaphanous cotton that undulate in the breeze. Or subtle knits in natural fibers layered over leggings.

JACKET: Go for a loose, deconstructed blazer or an easy wrap.

SHOES: Sandals or flats, perhaps with a cork sole to fit the whole wine motif—unless of course you're in the mountains somewhere in Napa. In that case, riding boots are the way to go.

ACCESSORIES: A pretty scarf (Hermès) or some chunky wooden jewelry to offset your diaphanous layers will work exquisitely.

A TASTE OF TRIVIA

- *Pigeage* is the French term for stomping grapes in open tanks, à la Lucy and Ethel on the classic wine-making episode of *I Love Lucy*.
- Domaine de la Romanée-Conti in Burgundy, France, is one of the most famous vineyards in the world. In 2001 Sotheby's sold a lot consisting of seven bottles of their Montrachet 1978 for $23,929 per bottle.

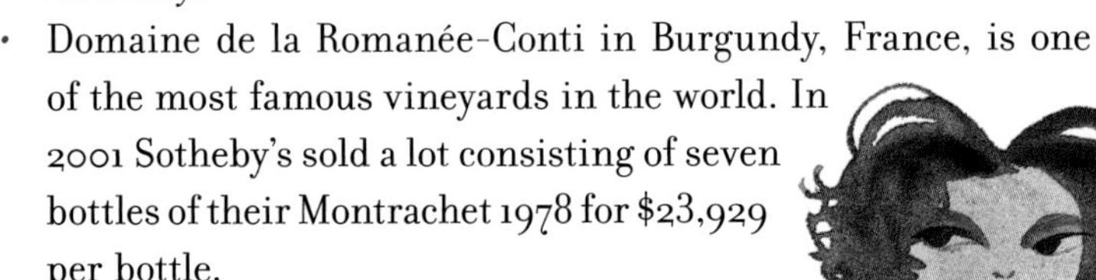

- The 1947 Château Cheval Blanc is one of the most desired wines of the twentieth century. (It even got a mention in the animated film *Ratatouille*.)

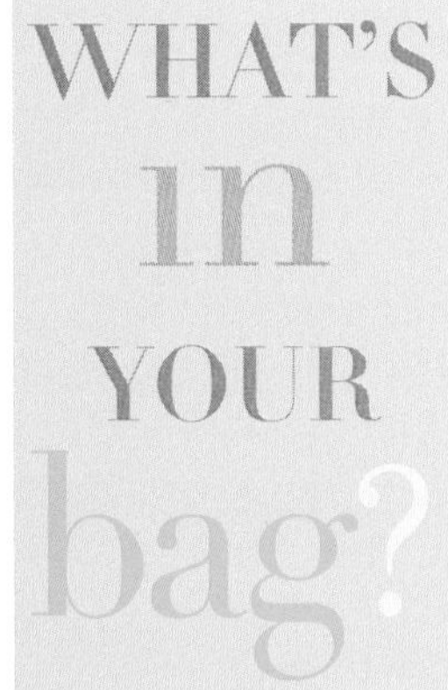

Make sure you have the number of a car service on your cell. The vino can sneak up on you.

All of life is a dispute over taste and tasting.

FRIEDRICH NIETZSCHE

A GLASS A DAY KEEPS THE DOCTOR AWAY

- A glass of wine a day will sharpen a woman's mind later in life. Cheers!
- Resveratrol found in red wine *might* help prevent heart disease, cancer, and obesity. "Might" is good enough for me.
- A red wine bath is said to be AMAZING for your skin. Sounds pricey to me, and not all that cleansing.

Glam Rock

What to Wear to a Rock Concert

I always thought I should be treated like a star.

MADONNA

Here's your chance to rock the garments in your closet that you may not have the courage to wear to a party or a dinner. This is the time to showcase your wild side.

Think edgy, punk rocker chic. Push your look to the limit. (Unless you're going to hear adult contemporary or light rock, in which case, I hate to say it, but you're on your own.) The first two words that come to mind when thinking of rock show attire are *denim* and *leather*. Build your ensemble around those iconically cool fabrics and you're guaranteed to look smashing. Rock and fashion have always had an intimate relationship; the rock star not dating or married to a model is the exception. Music icons have always danced along the cutting edge of style with teenagers eagerly following along. And the fashion world pays attention. If you are horrified by some new trend you see strolling through the local mall or walking out the door on your own teenage daughter, get ready to see a modified version of this trend on the catwalk in six months. The lines between fashion and music get blurrier every day, so approach concert wear as a peek into your own fashion future. By that I mean be daring and try something new.

Do not revisit the ubiquitous punk rock makeover straight out of an eighties teen movie. Avoid anything resembling a zebra-striped muscle shirt, spray-on pink hair color, black lipstick, and torn jeans held together with safety pins. If you take this route, you'll be in contention for Rock Fashion Disaster of the Year. You can do so much better.

> *Sometimes you have to sacrifice*
> *your performance for high heels.*
>
> GWEN STEFANI

rule breakers we love

Kate Moss

Kate Moss embodies hip, effortless rock style. Everything she wears looks as though it were made just for her and for that occasion. She's the girl who's dating the lead singer of the band. She'll mix distressed denim with sequins and stilettos. She understands balance and walks the tightrope between approachable and iconic without missing a step.

Aside from that bad eighties look, your options are limitless. Wear what makes you feel the beat, feel free, and feel like dancing. Skinny jeans, booties, and a cute, oversized off-the-shoulder T-shirt make a great foundation. Add funky earrings and a touch of glitter on your eyelids, and you're ready to rock.

What You Should Wear

PANTS: Leather is the ultimate in sexy, rocker chic. These pants should look and feel like a second skin. If you can, get a pair custom made; believe me, they're worth the investment. They never go out of style. They'll be an heirloom you can pass down for generations. But if leather isn't your bag, you still have endless options: jeans, a denim mini, or any number of synthetic leather substitutes.

TEE: Something edgy, with embellishments, an unusual cut, a cool graphic print, or all of the above. An oversize, off-the-shoulder top with a low-slung belt is always a great look.

OUTERWEAR: A funky faux fur vest or a great leather jacket.

SHOES: Converse, stilettos, knee- or thigh-high boots are all rocktastic, and all look fabulous with pants or a skirt.

The Ornaments

We cannot forget accessories. A studded, chunky belt, or two or three skinny belts in different colors, will look great with a tunic or oversize tee. Don't wear your grandmother's antique diamond earrings tonight; a rowdy crowd calls for jewelry that won't become a tragedy if it's lost. Bangles, cuffs, leather, rhinestones? Pile them on. As you dress, listen to the band you're about to see, dance around your bedroom, and practice your fist pump. Imagine how great this band will sound live. Now go out and rock it, but give yourself a quick edit before you walk out that door. And make sure you have your tickets!

Rock is all about writing your own script; it's all about pioneering.

COURTNEY LOVE

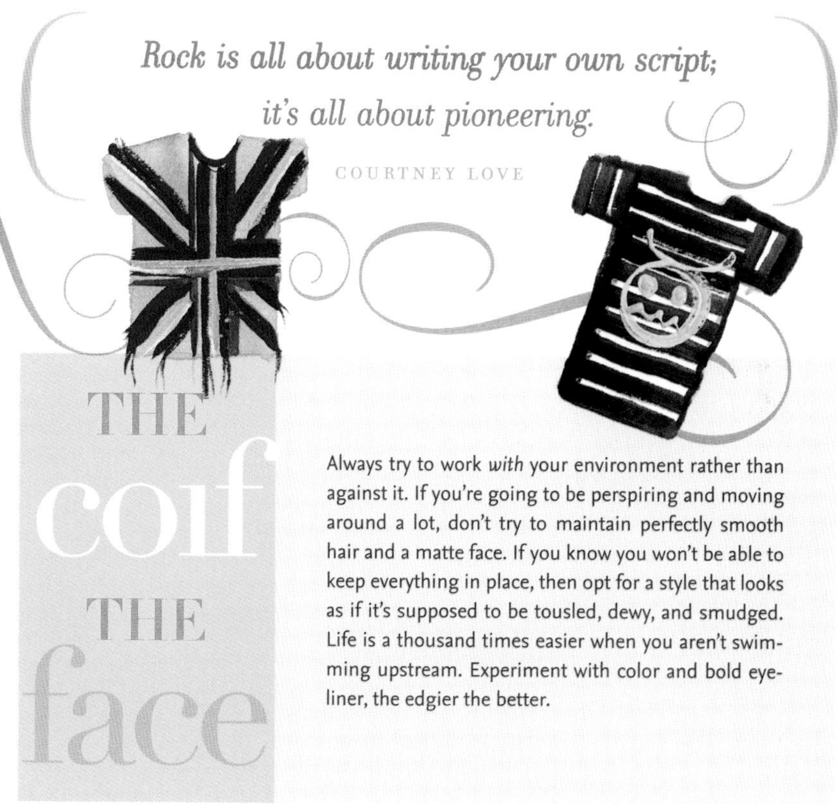

THE coif THE face

Always try to work *with* your environment rather than against it. If you're going to be perspiring and moving around a lot, don't try to maintain perfectly smooth hair and a matte face. If you know you won't be able to keep everything in place, then opt for a style that looks as if it's supposed to be tousled, dewy, and smudged. Life is a thousand times easier when you aren't swimming upstream. Experiment with color and bold eyeliner, the edgier the better.

THE COOL CROWD: ROCK AT ANY AGE

- TEENS: Taylor Momsen pushes her teenage rock and roll style to the limit. Most parents would not let her out of the house in some of her barely there skirts with visible garter belt ensembles, but she makes her sexy, sloppy, WTF attitude work.
- TWENTIES: Rihanna is fearless. She's not afraid to completely change her look or try extreme styles.
- THIRTIES: Indie style queen Karen O is always eclectic and cutting edge.
- FORTIES: Sheryl Crow epitomizes laid-back cool. She looks like she was born in faded jeans, a plaid shirt, and tousled hair, with a guitar over her shoulder.
- FIFTIES: Madonna is THE style chameleon of her generation and she continues to evolve and push the envelope flawlessly.
- SIXTIES: Cher will embody rock-and-roll glam to her grave.

Music is the mediator between the spiritual and the sensual life.

LUDWIG VAN BEETHOVEN

BE DARING

Think sexy and fun. Wear a lacy, colorful bra with straps you'd want peeking out now and then. This is the moment to pull out that fuchsia push-up you're so crazy about.

La Vogue Bohème

What to Wear to the Opera

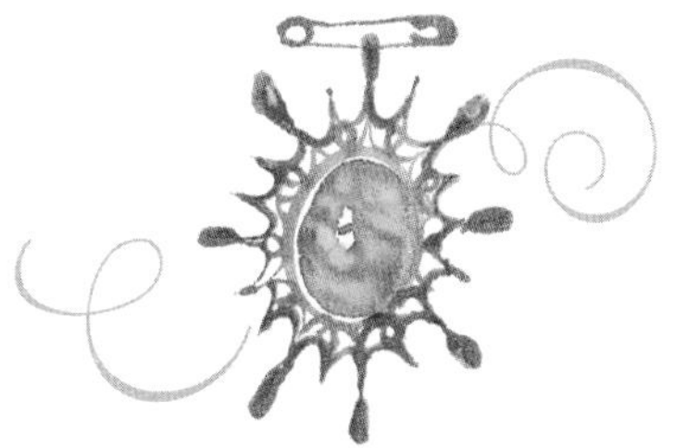

I have always believed that opera is a planet
where the muses work together,
join hands and celebrate all the arts.

FRANCO ZEFFIRELLI

In our increasingly casual society, there is no longer a hard-and-fast dress code for the opera. Audience attire runs the gamut from jeans and skirts to evening dresses and furs. Your options are limitless. But if you are going to a beautiful theater to see a beautiful performance, why not dress for it? Save the jeans for tomorrow's brunch (hopefully with your handsome date), and think about how you're going to doll it up tonight.

Semiformal dressing is always more fun than formal, so that's my recommendation for the evening. Opera is about romance and excess—excess emotion, ornate costumes, insanely talented singers, tragic love stories, and all things gilt and red and jewel-encrusted. Onstage there will be corseted bodices, voluminous velvet skirts, and gold braids. Offstage, take those theatrics down a few notches to create a look that's wearable and fierce.

Put a contemporary twist on old-school opera attire. Wear a gorgeous

I don't need the money, dear. I work for art.

MARIA CALLAS

velvet (but not crushed velvet) dress; adorn yourself with a few bright baubles and with gold shoes that have just a hint of metallic sheen. Or try a brocade opera coat over a long, narrow, beautifully tailored silk dress. Or mix vintage with cutting edge to evoke your favorite operatic heroine, such as Mimi, Violetta, Carmen, Isolde; take your pick and roll your look in her direction.

Just like at the theater and the art opening, people-watching at the opera can be as riveting as the actual performance, so arrive early to enjoy the spectacle. You'll get two costume dramas for the price of one. And remember, you're part of the pre-show cast. Make a regal entrance, look around with a Mona Lisa smile, and glide slowly to your seat as you carefully remove your gloves.

rules are made to be broken

Never mix metals.

What better place to mix your metals and indulge in the opulence than at the opera? Give your vintage pieces an edgy twist by mixing silver and gold; choose one to be your primary element and use the other metal as an accent.

OPERA GLOVES: WE LOVE!

Opera gloves are striking, edgy, and elegant. Traditionally they are made of white, black, or ivory kid leather. They are between nine and thirteen inches in length and very fitted, with an opening at the wrist and three buttons. In the past, it was considered unseemly to put them on or remove them in public. Picture a burlesque dancer slowly removing her gloves. Sexy.

Smoke and Mirrors

What to Wear to a Club—Comedy, Jazz, Magic . . .

Cock your hat—angles are attitudes.

FRANK SINATRA

I sometimes long for the days when we wouldn't dream of going to a club without glamming it up. Those halcyon days when smoking wasn't bad for you, girls were girls, and boys were boys. *Mad Men* has had a fabulous effect on the way young men approach formality; grunge is out and a suit-and-tie look is cool! Nonetheless, you can still get into most clubs wearing jeans and a T-shirt. My rule is: If you have to pay a cover charge, the venue merits some glitz.

When everyone is seated at tables enjoying appetizers and cocktails, the audience creates an ambiance for the show—it's only right that you do your part. You'll help the performer by looking like the style diva that you are. Being a vision of fashion loveliness is a responsibility. I expect you to live up to it.

Major Cities—Mega Clubs

Comedy in New York City

- Improv: Upright Citizens Brigade, the Magnet, the PIT
- Comic Strip Live: the oldest stand-up comedy showcase in the world
- Carolines

Comedy in Los Angeles

- Upright Citizens Brigade Theater
- The Groundlings
- Laugh Factory
- The Comedy Store

Comedy in Chicago

- The Second City: the birthplace of *SNL*

Jazz in New York City

- Birdland
- Blue Note
- Lenox Lounge
- Smalls
- Village Vanguard

Las Vegas is where the magic happens

- Just visit a Web site like vegas.com and see a listing of the latest magic acts.

What You Should Wear

CIGARETTE PANTS OR A PENCIL SKIRT: Picture Audrey Hepburn (I know she's mentioned a lot when discussing style, but there's a reason!) in *Funny Face* wearing a black turtleneck, black cigarette pants, and ballet flats. Gamine, beatnik; thank you, Givenchy.

TOP: A turtleneck as mentioned above, a constructed blouse, or a furry angora sweater (a perfectly innocent way to enhance your bust).

JACKET: I'm not sure why, but going to clubs seems like a winter activity, so you'll need a jacket or coat. Wear something unexpected and cool, or play it safe with a trench.

SHOES: If you choose to go full-on Audrey, then ballet flats are a must. Or wear a downtown-worthy shoe that straddles the line between edgy and pretty.

ACCESSORIES: A fedora will top off your outfit beautifully; a beret might be cute, but if you ask me, that's taking the beat theme a little too far. Cinch your waist with a wide belt and wear simple, metal jewelry. No bangles! Every clamorous gesture will result in a bevy of dirty looks.

rule breakers we love

Billie Holliday

The ultimate jazz icon. Beautiful, tragic, haunting. Beauty and tragedy are an irresistible combination, but you don't need to actually experience tragedy to embody the depth and pathos of Billie Holliday. The key is to know yourself, be yourself, and express yourself. The clothes are just accent pieces to highlight your inner complexity.

I confess that live stand-up comedy is not my favorite form of entertainment. When it's good, it's fabulous. But when it's bad, my heart breaks for the poor comedian, all alone on the stage, delivering jokes to dead air.

And my heart also breaks for *us*, the audience members, shrinking into our seats, collectively suffering through the humiliation. I shudder just thinking about it.

Live jazz is a different story. Over the years, a dear friend of mine, himself a jazz musician, has taken me on a wonderful tour of New York City's premier jazz venues. These legendary old clubs, steeped in nostalgia, are an amazing piece of entertainment history. Hearing a jazz great perform in a club like the Village Vanguard transports you back to the fifties, when this music was fresh and when new cultural ideas were crackling in the air like the beautifully dizzy melodies playing in the club. Nothing compares to it. It's well worth the watery $15 highballs.

> *I never go out unless I look like Joan Crawford the movie star. If you want to see the girl next door, go next door.*
>
> JOAN CRAWFORD

CLUBLAND ETIQUETTE *DON'TS*

- DON'T CHUCKLE KNOWINGLY in the silence between jazz riffs. You're not fooling anyone.
- DON'T CLAP ALONG TO THE MUSIC. I am not kidding. When I went to hear sax legend Lou Donaldson, a man clapped along (completely out of rhythm) the WHOLE time. It was awkward, to say the least.
- DON'T SIT NEAR THE STAGE at a comedy club if you're shy. Comedians can smell a reluctant victim a mile away.

Style in Motion

What to Wear to Go Dancing

Dance is the hidden language of the soul.

MARTHA GRAHAM

What is more fun than going dancing? Nothing I can think of. Unfortunately it's harder and harder to fit a night of dancing into my schedule (which saddens me to no end). If you can find the time for a night of tripping the light fantastic, you absolutely must do it. Dancing invigorates your senses in a way few activities can. If you cannot get out and go dancing with friends on a regular basis, enroll in a dance class immediately, especially if you're single; you might just meet the man of your dreams and love might blossom with each kick-ball-change. *And* you'll be the belle of the ball the next time you and the girls do head out dancing.

I know the terms *discotheque* and *disco dancing* are outdated, but I also adore how they evoke the spirit of Studio 54 in its heyday, an era of glam excess at its most fashionably fabulous—a great inspiration to keep in mind when putting together your outfit.

Dance first. Think later. It's the natural order.

SAMUEL BECKETT

For Partnered Dances, Such as Salsa, Mambo, or Swing

Wear a flowy, flouncy skirt that swirls around you as you twirl. Combine this skirt with a fitted top, put on a gorgeous, wide belt to accentuate your waist, and you will look like the dancing queen you are. ABBA, we love you.

To a Club

Although we're currently living in a more subdued time, dance attire is still pretty much anything goes. Whatever makes you want to get your freak on, as they say, is fair game. A select few can get away with spandex pants à la Olivia Newton-John's *Grease* makeover ensemble. Go for it if your derriere is up to the task. The rest of us, those with more curvaceous figures, should wear anything that sparkles and dazzles.

Remember to step into footwear you can dance in, preferably a strappy pair of heels or high-heeled booties. No matter which kind of dance you do, you can't move your hips as well in flats. It's true!

UNDERNEATH it all

GARTERS AND SCENT

Feel saucy? A quick glimpse of your garter belt as you turn will be absolutely intoxicating. Add a sexy, musky fragrance such as Yves Saint Laurent's Opium

Finally, be a little daring. No, be a lot daring. Dance like no one is watching you. Practice your natural sense of rhythm and a certain amount of coordination; both will be key when you hit the floor. But the only thing you really need to be a dancing queen is Confidence with a capital C. If you glide out to the middle of an empty dance floor and start moving as if your favorite song is playing, you're having a fantastic time, and you don't have a care in the world, the dance floor won't be empty for long. Be the magnet. And make sure your cosmetics are sweatproof.

SALSA

Salsa dancing is one of my favorite styles of dance, with its Afrocentric rhythm and upbeat, Caribbean sentiment. I love the beat, the music, the moves, and if a woman has a good partner, she needs to know only the basics to work it like a pro. This is one case where it's much harder to be a man (he has to lead the whole time), so take advantage, ladies.

Salsa Classics

- Celia Cruz, "Quimbara"
- Frankie Negrón, "Comerte a besos"
- Gilberto Santa Rosa, "La Conciencia"
- Marc Anthony, "Te conozco bien"
- Orquesta Guayacán, "Invierno en primavera"
- Rey Ruiz, "Creo en el amor"
- Richie Ray, "Sonido bestial"
- Rubén Blades, "Siembra"
- Salserín, "Una fan enamorada"
- Tito Gómez, "Página de amor"

rule breakers we love

Josephine Baker

She broke rules and shattered the status quo. And who else could look so good in a banana skirt? Josephine Baker is a great example of a woman who knew how to make the most of her assets. She had the courage to express her style and ignore the critics and stale social mores.

holidays

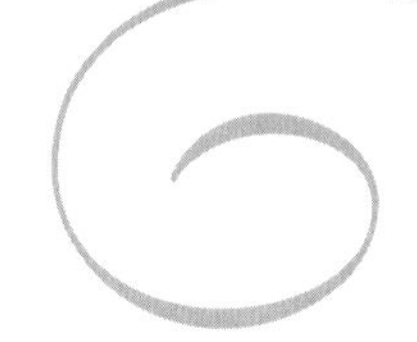

Style Resolution

What to Wear to a New Year's Eve Party

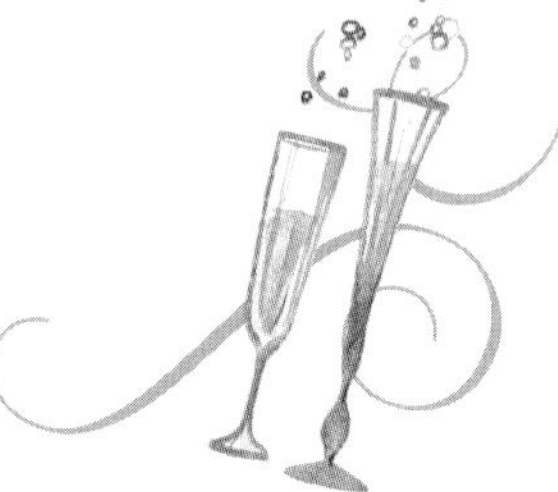

Women are women, and hurray for that.

JOHN GALLIANO

New Year's Eve is my favorite holiday to dress for. It's all about festivity, conviviality, and excess. Champagne bubbles throughout the night and there's a delightful New Year's Eve buzz, with perhaps somebody to kiss at midnight, and coming home with a nest of confetti in your hair. Sublime. Plus this is an occasion that you cannot overdress for. More is more. *Go* with it.

Whether your biggest New Year's Eve challenge is deciding how many parties you can fit into the evening or figuring out a way to get your sweetheart off the couch and into *one* great party, you want to make sure you get to your chosen destination in time to toast the stroke of midnight. It's so anticlimactic to ring in the New Year while stuck in traffic on your way to a fabulous party. Needless to say, your ensemble has to carry you from cocktail hour through midnight—and if you're really having a great time, you won't have a moment to spare for changes, even quick ones; so choose wisely and make sure of two critical things before you go out: one, that you're comfortable, and two, that you absolutely adore how you look.

Extravagance is the rule. What better occasion than New Year's Eve

to drape yourself in gold and silver lamé? Bedeck yourself in jewels, wrap yourself in sparkle, and shine. Aim for glamorous, not garish; don't pile items on for the sake of piling them on. Think accents. Wear strappy stilettos. I prefer a knee-length dress unless an event is ultra formal, but a micromini with tights is great if you've got the legs. (Floor length could be too dressy unless you're attending a formal dinner.)

New Year's Eve is the one occasion when your little black cocktail dress should not be your fallback choice. You can never go *seriously* wrong with your trusty LBD, but wearing black on New Year's Eve is a bit like wearing a tasteful sheath to Mardi Gras. *Why?* You have free rein to go full glam tonight, so work it. (If you must wear black, try to find something with beading or sequins, add a burst of color with accessories and leg wear, or at least put on a festive wrap.)

Be playful, channel your inner Edie Sedgwick—she always looked smashing and ready to be the life of the party.

One term that often comes up in conversations about what ought to be one of the most special nights of the year is "anticlimactic." People complain that their evening wasn't all that it was hyped up to be; disappointment sets in. Sometimes it sets in at 11:30 that night, and sometimes it creeps in the next day at brunch when you realize the best part of your New Year's celebration just might be the chocolate croissant that you're about to devour. Well, to all that I say: Don't have an anticlimactic New Year's Eve! If you look amazing, you'll feel amazing; and if you look and feel amazing, you're guaranteed to have an amazing night.

What You Should Wear

SEPARATES: You have so many options. High-waisted satin pants with a lean cut, tuxedos, harem, sequin leggings. Pair them with a dressy tank and a gorgeous jacket. You can even wear jeans if that's what you fancy. A sexy silk or satin jumpsuit is also an easy and comfortable choice.

DRESS: A festive, sexy cocktail dress, probably strapless and definitely glamorous. This is a once-a-year über-showstopping look. So find the perfect, perfect party dress that looks amazing on you. Trimming, beading, sequins, feathers; whatever gives you that extra zest. Show some skin with a plunging décolletage or a micromini (choose one or the other, both can look a bit tarty). A standout frock with modern adornment like an origami detail, an architectural bodice, or an unusual cut is always a head turner. If you prefer a dress with more traditional lines, then try an unusual fabric—leather is fantastic and unexpected in a dress—anything that has a little something to set it apart.

JACKET: Something with sequins or faux fur. Your jacket should be as special and fancy as your frock.

SHOES: Sky-high heels; pretty, funky, party shoes like Charlotte Olympia or Jean-Michel Cazabat. You can rest your feet the next morning over a scrumptious egg and bacon sandwich.

ACCESSORIES: Go for extravagant bijouterie, such as a statement necklace and/or loads of bangles. If it sparkles and shines, and makes you feel fancy, wear it. If you think it might be a raucous night, stick with costume gems.

BAG: Pick a beautiful jewel of a bag; clutch, evening, or minaudière.

THE coif THE face

Tonight of all nights, your hair and makeup should be as ravishing as your ensemble. I like my hair down and a bit tousled. A dramatic eye, the lightest dusting of glittery face powder, and juicy, just-kissed lips will set off your party look brilliantly.

The bottom line on dressing for New Year's Eve is that planning and shopping for just the right outfit is half the fun. When you find something that makes you feel like a star, you've got your ensemble. It should give you the urge to run out and show off your stellar look.

Edie Sedgwick is such a perfect party-style role model because she had the ability to make whatever she happened to have on look as though she had bought it specifically for wherever she happened to be. Even before Lady Gaga's pantless excursions about town, Edie was dancing the night away in leotards and tights. She'd toss on a leopard coat, throw on some stilettos, do her signature doe-eye, and look stunning. Follow her dynamic lead.

Dress up or down as you see fit. The New Year's Eve color palette is anything goes, so if you love vivid hues and bold patterns, have fun with them. If you love black, work the textures and finishes. Always remember, Edie was an heiress who could afford couture yet she wore leotards to the most fabulous New York bashes; so even if you can't afford the crème de la crème, with a little ingenuity you can put together something just as showstopping.

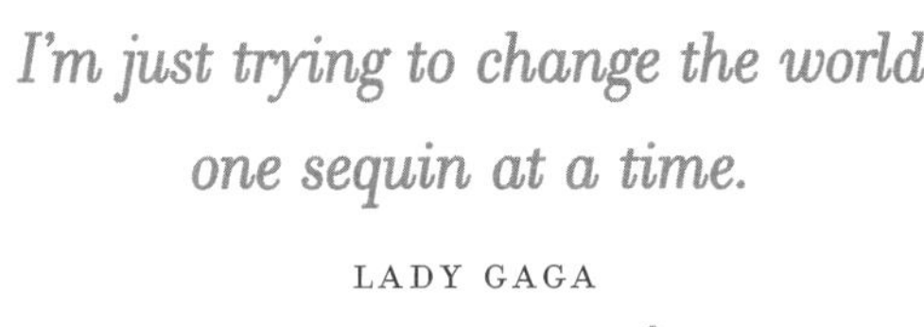

NINA'S TOP FIVE NEW YEAR'S STYLE RESOLUTIONS

GET YOUR FINANCES IN ORDER. It's the same every year but we all have to try, right?

BE GREENER. Eco-friendly and fashion forward are not mutually exclusive. Explore some of the green styles out there.

TRY NEW CLOTHING COMBOS. Be a lifelong fashion learner. Keep your look fresh by mixing and matching. You won't have to shop nearly as much.

POSTURE. Good posture is essential. It makes you appear taller, thinner, stronger, and CONFIDENT.

RULES ARE MADE TO BE BROKEN. Need I say more?

Now, go buy some streamers and confetti and remember that the key concept for your New Year's Eve ensemble is effervescence. The New Year is a moment of endless possibilities, a time to begin writing new chapters in your life. So go out and dance until dawn, make your resolutions, and don't start trying to fulfill any of them until January 2. Maybe even January 3. It all depends on how much champagne you've had.

rule breakers we love

Lady Gaga

Lady Gaga challenges our concept of fashion, theater, beauty, and glamour while embodying sexy femininity. I realize that few women have the courage (or the desire) to dress like Gaga, but we should all take a page from her book when it comes to pushing our own style limits and trying to view the classics in a thoroughly modern way. She's a walking fantasy. I can't wait to see what she dreams up next.

Hangover Chic

What to Wear to New Year's Day Brunch

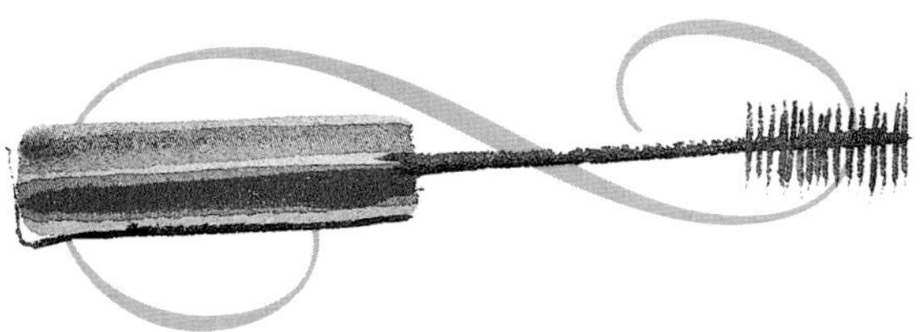

There is no end. There is no beginning.
There is only the passion of life.

FEDERICO FELLINI

What's the perfect antidote to New Year's Eve debauchery? New Year's Day Brunch, of course. Bloody Marys and mimosas are the first order of business, followed by a strong cup of coffee and a delicious, carb-loaded meal to kick off the New Year on the right note.

Unfortunately, you have to get dressed before indulging in any of these palliatives. I advise you to choose an outfit the day before and have it laid out and ready to go as soon as you step out of the shower, hopefully no earlier than noon. After the festivities of the previous night, easy and relaxed should be the style rule on this day. Welcome the New Year with good friends, good food, and a comfortable and fantastic outfit.

What You Should Wear

TROUSERS: Men's style, wool trousers are cozy, a little dressier than jeans, and they evoke images of eating a meal in front of a roaring fire with snow on the ground outside. Or if you want to offset the bulkiness of the sweater, you can opt for fitted corduroys. Jane Fonda had scrumptious figure-conscious sweater/pants combos in *Barefoot in the Park.*

SWEATER: It's January so you've *got* to wear a sweater. A yummy cashmere piece or a fisherman's sweater are true classics; they're warm, roomy, and give you a hug on the first day of the year. Why not go shopping in your boyfriend's/husband's closet?

SHOES: Loafers or desert shoes with trousers, or riding boots over fitted cords.

If you can't make it good,
at least make it look good.

BILL GATES

DRESSING FOR NEW YEAR LUCK

Make It Good!

- WEAR RED. It symbolizes prosperity and wealth. And it's a great accent color.
- WEAR SOMETHING NEW. This will ensure that your year is filled with new clothes. And who doesn't love new clothes?
- DON'T BORROW OR LEND ANYTHING. New Year's Day sets the tone for the next twelve months, so if you borrow, you will be borrowing all year, and if you lend, you'll be lending all year. That *probably* also means you should avoid a one-night stand.

EATING FOR LUCK

A great variety of foods are considered good luck. These are some fairly universal and delicious choices.

- EAT TWELVE GRAPES AT THE STROKE OF MIDNIGHT. They symbolize the months of the year and bring good fortune.
- COOKED GREENS: Their leafy greenness represents money and health.
- BEANS, PEAS, OR LENTILS ARE COMMON NEW YEAR'S DAY FOODS AROUND THE WORLD. They symbolize money or coins. In the United States black-eyed peas are a Southern New Year's tradition.
- PORK: Pigs eat while moving forward, so their meat symbolizes progress and prosperity. Fish is also a lucky New Year's Day food for this reason.
- DOUGHNUTS, OR A DOUGHNUT-SHAPED CAKE, ARE A CROSS-CULTURAL DESSERT ON NEW YEAR'S DAY. Often with a surprise or two baked inside.
- STAY AWAY FROM WINGED FOWL on New Year's Day, as they represent your luck flying away. LOBSTER symbolizes your luck retreating, so that's a no-no too.

THE coif THE face

Keep your hair and makeup natural and fresh, with a little bit of color on your cheeks for a New Year glow. Let your hair down on this day. After a good cleansing, comb some leave-in conditioner into your hair. Fresh year, fresh you. A little mascara, don't forget some lip stain, and you're done.

Reality Bites

What to Wear If You're Single on Valentine's Day

If you don't love yourself, how in the hell you gonna love somebody else?

RUPAUL

We've all been there: Valentine's Day without a significant other. If this happens to you, do remember that you're not alone. When you don't have a romantic evening planned, gather your single girlfriends and go have a good time. There's absolutely no reason to sit at home feeling sorry for yourself. Chances are that you and the girls will have more fun than almost every one of those irritating couples with their candlelight dinners and boxes of chocolates (all items I love, by the way, but when you're single not so much). Get dressed up, go out, have a ball, and don't even talk about men. Or stay home, give each other facials and manicures, and only talk about men. Forget the holiday and do some female bonding.

I say it's a girls' world.

NELLY FURTADO

What You Should Wear

JEANS: Skinny, distressed, or embellished jeans; anything that looks good on me and has a little bit of an edge. You bring out your favorite gear; whatever makes you feel like a beautiful woman. If you aren't in the mood for jeans, and the tunic is long enough, wear leggings. Or throw on an easy dress in a fun print, add a pair of tights, and you're ready to go.

TOP: A loose tunic with dolman sleeves; I'm thinking silk, with embroidery around the neck and hem. Add a low-slung belt. Underneath, wear a tank or a fitted turtleneck. If it's very chilly out, keep the turtleneck, lose the tunic, and go for a bulky knitted vest with a belt.

COAT: February is usually cold, so bundle up in a fabulous wool trench and a warm hat.

SHOES: Knee- or thigh-high boots. Putting on fierce boots is an instant pick-me-up.

ACCESSORIES: A charm bracelet for good vibes or a cuff to channel the warrior. Oversize hoop earrings or some chandeliers will add a bit of sparkle.

rule breakers we love

Jennifer Aniston

She's not a fashion rule breaker, by any means, but her classic style highlights her tawny good looks. The tabloids have turned Jennifer Aniston into the unwilling poster girl for the lovelorn. If she's an example of unlucky in love, then girls everywhere should be clamoring to be single.

Aim for girlie and romantic to maintain that little spark. You have to be sending out those subliminal messages if you want to stay in the romance game. Or just be silly; the best gag underwear I've ever seen was briefs with a big heart on the hip that said, "All this and brains too." Hilarious.

GIRL POWER

Sisters Are Doing It for Themselves

- EXCHANGE SILLY GIFTS. Give each other ridiculously cheap and questionable lingerie on Valentine's Day. It's part encouragement to "go there" and part "why do we care so much about this holiday of the heart." Instant laughs.
- DO SOMETHING COMPLETELY GIRL-CENTRIC. Go see a chick flick, have a mini swap party, throw a slumber party (with cocktails).
- HAVE EVERYONE RAID THE NEAREST SEPHORA. Pool the beauty booty and give each other makeovers.
- FLOWERS AND CHOCOLATE ARE A MUST. Dark chocolate is healthy, so go ahead and eat a ton of it.

You must go out feeling like the ravishing creature you are. Dress for fun, not to impress anyone. Dress for yourself.

Love-In

What to Wear to Valentine's Dinner with a Significant Other

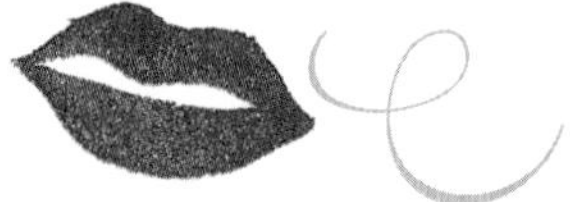

When love is not madness, it is not love.

PEDRO CALDERÓN DE LA BARCA

Valentine's Day is one of *those* holidays. You're under a crazy amount of pressure to have the most romantic, most wonderful evening ever—the stress can get slightly out of hand. Remember to put things into perspective; it's only one night and, truth be told, it doesn't mean all that much. Yes, it's an opportunity to celebrate your romance, but it's still only one night.

You know your friends are going to demand a recap the next day. The girls will want to know what he got you, where he took you, if he brought you roses, and if he did bring you roses, how many and what color. When your relationship is brand new, Valentine's Day becomes a test to determine how serious he is. For many of us women, romantic tokens and sincerity count for a lot during courtship, and if there was ever a day to exchange those tokens, Valentine's Day is it.

On the flip side, men are so aware of our expectations that it's almost crippling for them. Some rebel by refusing to follow the prescribed traditions (thereby hurting your feelings whether you want to admit it or not), while others go the whole nine yards (which can freak you out a bit at the beginning of a relationship, but you feel obligated to appreciate, resulting in guilt followed by anger). Either way, Valentine's Day is almost too much for the fragile seedling of new love to bear.

I ♥ VALENTINE'S DAY

Eighty-five percent of Valentine's cards are purchased by women and 64 percent of men don't make special Valentine's Day plans. Like I said, ladies, there's nothing wrong with taking charge of the holiday and planning your night, if it's important to you. The majority of us do anyway, just for the fun of it. It's a playful way to ritualize romance, so throw on an old Sade record and let yourself get sexy.

My recommendation for young lovers on February 14? Plan ahead. Don't hope he's going to sweep you off your feet. He might, and that's wonderful. But if he doesn't, don't read into it! It will only taint your burgeoning romance, or dent an existing one. Take charge; you're a modern woman. Plan the evening yourself; give your man a treat. Cook him dinner and spend the evening in, getting to know each other better. If you don't cook, order takeout. Gourmet takeout, of course. Light some candles, have a little wine, and make it a delightful, relaxing evening.

If you've been together for years, Valentine's Day is the perfect opportunity to fall in love all over again. Take this evening to reconnect, spend some quality time together.

> *To me there is no greater courage than being the one who kisses first.*
>
> JANEANE GAROFALO

What You Should Wear

SEPARATES: A silky pair of pajama-style pants are a luxurious option for a romantic evening in. Combine them with an adorable tank or a pretty knit top.

DRESS: Something slightly dressy but body conscious and sexy; and maybe even a little bit sweet. Think clingy, soft, figure hugging, and touchable such as cashmere or silk, along the lines of a Diane von Furstenberg wrap dress. Wear fabrics that feel good against your skin (and his). Go as fancy or as casual as you want, as long as you feel like a goddess.

COAT: If you do go out for dinner, a coat is in order. Choose something with a nod to the past. A feminine, vintage-inspired silhouette evokes tradition and romance.

SHOES: Romantic heels or fetching silk ballet flats.

ACCESSORIES: Keep it simple. Wear something that he gave you; if that's not an option (and it better be), wear anything that has sentimental value.

SEXY, SEXY LINGERIE: Sugar on the outside and spice on the inside. There's no better recipe for Valentine's night.

Your hair and makeup should be perfectly undone/done. Sweep your hair back into a loose knot or ponytail. No heavy liner on the eyes, just a sweep of brown or gray shadow and lashes for days, simple and smoldering. Add a dusting of luminous powder and sheer baby pink lips. You'll look fantastic and natural. Dab on your favorite perfume, fresh and floral or spicy and musky, whichever you fancy or whichever *he* fancies. Sizzle and simmer, don't boil.

UNDERNEATH it all

SAUCY FUN

A garter belt is a must. There's nothing sexier than stockings with a bit of milky thigh beneath a garter. Wear a full slip over your bra and panties to give him layers and layers of silky seduction. It's like unwrapping a beautiful present.

Finally, ladies, because this is the twenty-first century, surprise him with a little gift. We women are in charge of our own destiny, and we should embrace this. I love giving spontaneous, romantic presents to my husband now and then. It's unexpected and sweet and that look of love that you get is always worth it. There's no need to go all out, just a thoughtful token of your love.

Valentine's Day doesn't have to be a big production. Forget about the gender rules, ignore the peer pressure, and just take the time to say I love you (or I like you, if you haven't gotten there yet), and indulge in the sensual pleasures. Good food, good wine, good company, and good . . . well, you know.

rule breakers we love

Gypsy Rose Lee

Gypsy Rose Lee is the original burlesque queen. Learn from her, ladies. Her secret to seduction was a winning combination of flirtation and witty banter as she slowly shed her clothes. Never underestimate the allure of clever conversation; and we all know a little private striptease doesn't hurt.

In Washington, we know that spring has arrived when the White House lawn is filled with children for the Easter egg hunt.

LAURA BUSH

Spring Has Sprung

What to Wear for Easter Dinner

Isn't elegance forgetting what one is wearing?

YVES SAINT LAURENT

So many holidays, so little to wear. The more multicultural we become, the more holidays there are to celebrate. Fun—but it can be exhausting to dress for so many functions. Lucky for us, Easter and Passover occur around the same time of year, springtime. Understanding and appreciating the season is at least half the wardrobe battle for any event. Spring's arrival symbolizes rebirth, new life, and a new fashion cycle. In honor of these many blessings, make renewing and sharpening your look part of your personal spring holiday tradition.

True to the "go big or go home" philosophy in the United States (which does help make this country great), what began as a simple custom of buying a new hat for Easter has become a competition to see who can don the most decadently frilly chapeau. Blame Irving Berlin for writing the song, and the movie *Easter Parade* for bringing it to life for millions of viewers. Oh, go ahead and blame Judy Garland too. I myself say "No" to the overdecorated Easter bonnet, and "Absolutely yes" to wearing something new. It doesn't *have* to be a hat to fulfill the spirit of the tradition, it just has to be something you wear.

What You Should Wear

DRESS: It is fun to be at least a little bit frilly on Easter Sunday, so embrace your girliest-girl style on this day. Wear a gorgeous spring dress. Florals or pastels are a must; maybe even with ruffles or lace. I'm not encouraging you to dress like Bette Davis in *Whatever Happened to Baby Jane?* Just wear something cheerful and church appropriate, even if you don't plan to attend Easter services.

JACKET: You may need a light jacket or sweater, or a slicker to ward off the April showers. A light trench or a colorful, three-quarter-length windbreaker are wonderful options. Rodarte and Anna Sui do gorgeous, girlie, and always modern spring coats. Try playing with silhouette and volume, such as a full-skirted trench or an A-line windbreaker.

SHOES: Keep the girlie theme going. Wear Mary Janes, or sandals if weather permits. Don't forget a pedicure; your toes must make an impeccable spring debut.

ACCESSORIES: Modest accessories work perfectly with a frilly dress. You don't want to overdo the froufrou. Perhaps an heirloom brooch or a simple strand of pearls. And, of course, you can wear a hat—but not a bonnet! Please.

Keep your hair neat and smooth and your makeup young and fresh for Easter dinner. Sheer products are a foolproof way to rock a fun, colorful palette without looking like a clown.

I adore the tradition of a late afternoon Easter supper, but my favorite Easter activities are decorating eggs and creating the perfect Easter basket. One can become lost in the world of pretty, miniature pastel trinkets while making lifetime memories for the kids.

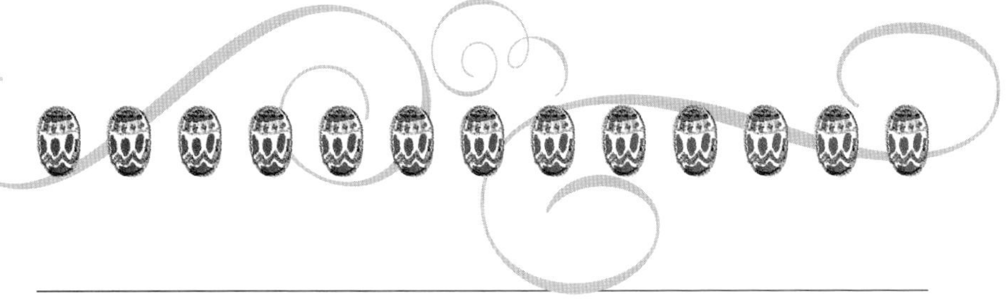

EASTER EGGS

Beyond the PAAS Easter Egg Kits, waaay beyond . . .

- FABERGÉ EGGS: Breathtaking, jewel-encrusted creations made by the House of Fabergé. In Imperial Russia, tiny Fabergé eggs were commonly exchanged as Easter gifts. These coveted baubles were worn as pendants and were considered quite a status symbol during this time. The larger eggs were custom-made for the Imperial Tsars Alexander III and Nicholas II of Russia. These are the extremely rare ones that are always being stolen in movies.
- UKRAINIAN EGGS: Actual, intact eggshells (the egg has been blown out) that have been dyed using a wax resist method, an ancient technique popular in many Eastern European countries. The decorative dye patterns are astonishingly intricate and beautiful.

Let My People Glow

What to Wear to a Passover Seder

There's nothing more life-affirming than sitting at a long table surrounded by friends and family going through the fifteen rituals (which include plenty of wine) in the Haggadah (more on this later) before digging into a feast. And best of all: There's not a dinner roll in sight; not even a bread stick, a scone, a muffin—or any other dangerous carb. On Passover, it's all things unleavened, so to those of you who live on some version of the Atkins diet, rejoice.

HELPFUL HINTS IF YOU'VE NEVER BEEN TO A PASSOVER SEDER

These tips will help you make it through your first Passover Seder faux pas–free.

- DON'T BRING BREAD. With the exception of matzo, all grains are forbidden on Passover.
- ONLY BRING FOOD OR WINE LABELED "KOSHER FOR PASSOVER." There are different kinds/levels of kosher.
- HAVE A SNACK BEFORE YOU LEAVE THE HOUSE. You won't be served dinner until after the Haggadah is read (and it can take a while).
- DON'T TOUCH THE SEDER PLATE. Just don't.

Isn't there any other part of the matzo you can eat?

MARILYN MONROE

Passover begins on the fourteenth day of Nisan in the Hebrew calendar (roughly March or April in the Gregorian calendar). It celebrates the exodus and subsequent freedom from slavery of the Children of Israel from Egypt. The Haggadah is a religious text that is read at the Passover Seder; it guides everyone through the story of Exodus and the accompanying rituals. While Passover is a very important religious holiday for the Jewish faith, much like Easter dinner for Christians, this meal is a celebration, and people of all faiths are welcome to take part. So be a mensch, break out the pocket Hebrew dictionary, and pull up a seat.

It's up to the host how formal the Passover dinner will be, but as a rule, it's more festive and family oriented than starched and buttoned-up.

What You Should Wear

DRESS: If you wore a dress for Easter dinner, go ahead and wear one tonight too. Rather than pastels, think about deeper colors (just to mix things up a bit), lean toward subtle stripes rather than florals, and simple elegance over frills. Of course, you can wear trousers, but I prefer a dress for this special dinner.

COAT: Put on a light blazer or fitted cotton jacket or a belted cardigan to stay warm on a brisk spring evening. Look at Temperley London's fanciful outerwear for some inspiration.

SHOES: Heels or pretty sandals. Celebrate spring with a new polish color on your toes.

ACCESSORIES: Accent your dress with a skinny belt if you're feeling prim or go with an extra-wide belt if you want a touch of sass. Add a delicate silver or gold cuff and a gauzy scarf and you're set.

THE FOUR QUESTIONS

Near the start of the Seder the youngest person at the table asks these four questions. Just to give you a little flavor of the evening.

1. Why do we eat matzo?
   To remember our ancestors who did not have time to let their bread rise before they fled Egypt.
2. Why do we eat bitter herbs?
   To remind us of the bitterness of slavery.
3. Why do we dip parsley in salt water?
   It symbolizes the tears of the slaves.
4. Why do we lean on a pillow during the meal?
   To symbolize the comforts of freedom.

It's a good thing that there's a certain amount of fasting around both Easter and Passover. With so much candy and so many sumptuous banquets, you're likely to go up at least one size on everything in your closet by the time summer rolls around. Do indulge in moderation; soak up the *spiritual* bounty. L'Chaim! (To Life!)

> *Passover affirms the great truth that liberty is the inalienable right of every human being.*
>
> MORRIS JOSEPH

Weekend Warrior

What to Wear on Memorial Day and Labor Day

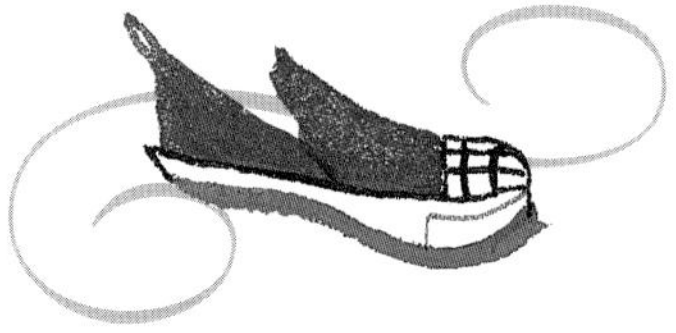

In my end is my beginning.

T. S. ELIOT

It amazes me that two long weekends, one during spring and the other in the fall, can be so loaded with meaning. Memorial Day, the last Monday in May, heralds the summer and all of that season's joy and leisure, while Labor Day, at the beginning of September, kicks us into the bustle of school and work and readying ourselves for the brisk winter to come. Both of these weekends arrive just when we're overdue for a change, which may be why people make fabulous plans for them.

rule breakers we love

Kathryn Bigelow

From *Point Break* to *The Hurt Locker*, director Kathryn Bigelow creates riveting action films—historically, a completely male-dominated genre. In 2010 she became the first woman to win an Academy Award for Best Director. The icing on the cake? She's stunning. Kathryn Bigelow is a wonderful example of a woman who works with "masculine" subject matter in a "masculine" field without having to be one of the boys. She's a woman's woman who has conquered a man's realm.

Memorial Day

Memorial Day originated after the Civil War as a day of remembrance for Americans killed in the line of duty. Despite its solemn origins, Memorial Day has come to represent the first of our summer jaunts and a much needed day off from work. Like many of you, I'm sure, my Memorial Day ensemble is all about relaxing for a long weekend at the beach. Set your worries aside, buy a stack of magazines or a steamy romance novel, and kick back. Perhaps make time for a cookout or a picnic for good measure.

Do pack a bag and take a quick getaway. Even if you can manage only a trip to a park or a hike in the mountains, you owe it to yourself to enjoy some ME time. Put together a look worthy of your day off, something superbly chic and laid back. If you don't have a BBQ to attend, invite a few friends over and host one yourself. Don't worry about pre-planning, use paper plates—no muss, no fuss. Nothing says summertime like the smell of burgers on the grill.

What You Should Wear

SEPARATES: White sailor pants look fabulous at the beach, but if you have kids or are cooking out, the risk of a spill might rule them out. Bermudas or a loose maxi dress are both fabulous alternatives. If you're ready to bare your legs so early in the season, go for it and wear a little sundress. Nicole Richie has weekend summer dressing perfected. For a sportier look, check out A.P.C.

JACKET: A boyfriend blazer, jean jacket, or light cardigan will keep you warm after the sun goes down.

SHOES: Sandals or sneaks. And don't forget about Havaianas and espadrilles—both are terrific summer shoes.

ACCESSORIES: Only the basics at the beach. You don't want to lose your priceless heirloom diamonds in the sand. A sturdy chain necklace or bracelet for a nautical touch, and a scarf are all you need.

BAG: A roomy tote for the beach; pack a casual clutch inside that doubles as a cosmetics bag and evening bag (in case you go out later).

Labor Day

Summer is almost over. Sigh. There's that crispness in the air and the leaves are starting to turn. Our beach vacations are coming to an end, and we have to start thinking of new plans as fall arrives, bringing school and cooler weather. Labor Day is bittersweet; we may as well make the most of it.

Labor Day actually originated in Canada—who knew? It's observed on the first Monday in September and is a celebration of the workingman and -woman. By now you've had your big summer vacay, and if you're me, Fall Fashion Week insanity is about to descend, with all its frenzy and spectacular clothing. So we've got to make this weekend extra fun and RELAXING.

Squeeze the last drops of serenity out of that time-share and make the most of your skin's summery glow and your hair's glistening golden highlights.

rules are made to be broken

Never wear white after Labor Day.

This rule was obviously enacted before we had such a fantastic variety of winter whites. White is modern, smart, and wearable year-round.

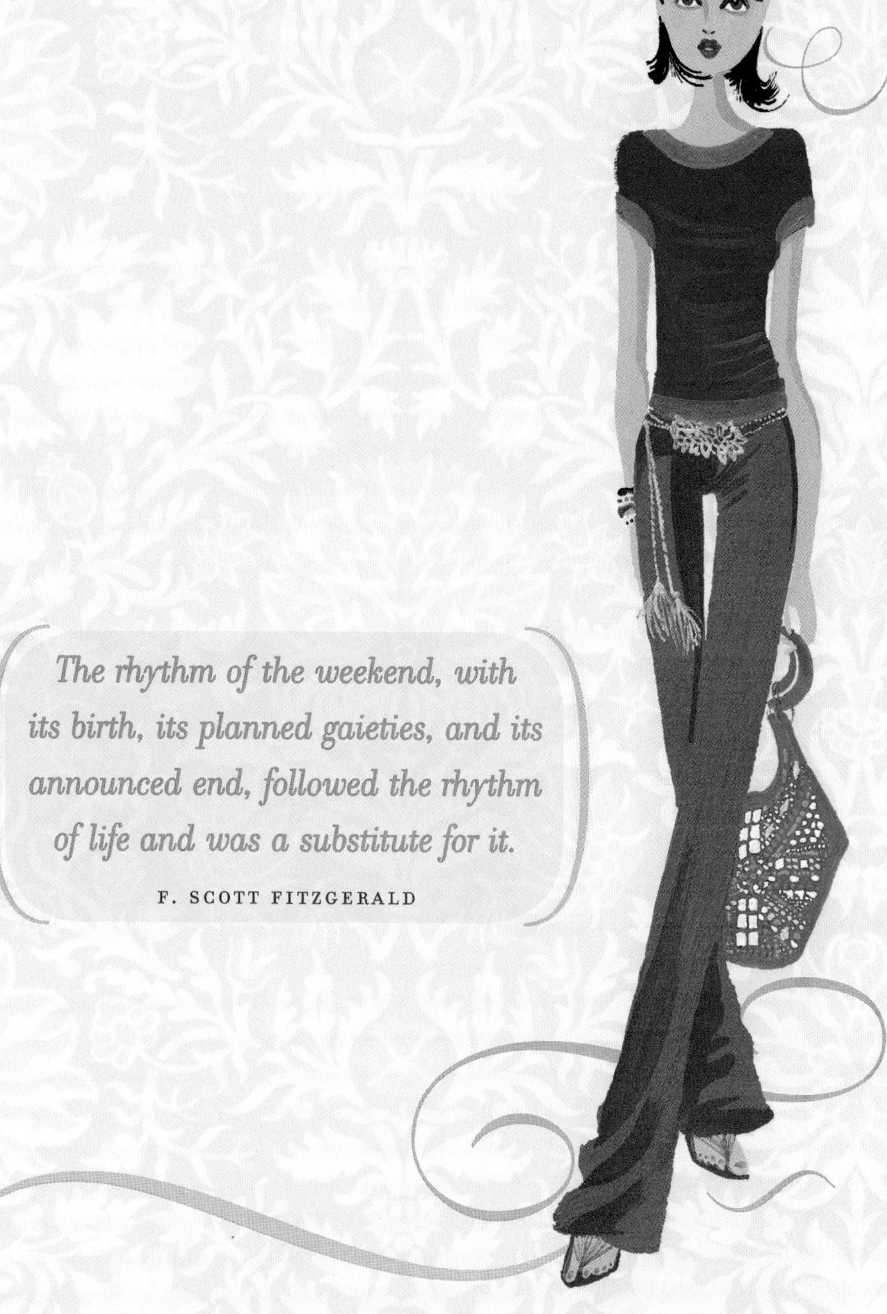

The rhythm of the weekend, with its birth, its planned gaieties, and its announced end, followed the rhythm of life and was a substitute for it.

F. SCOTT FITZGERALD

WHAT'S in YOUR bag?

Napkins, a compact, and sparklers.

Patriotic Panache

What to Wear to a Fourth of July Picnic

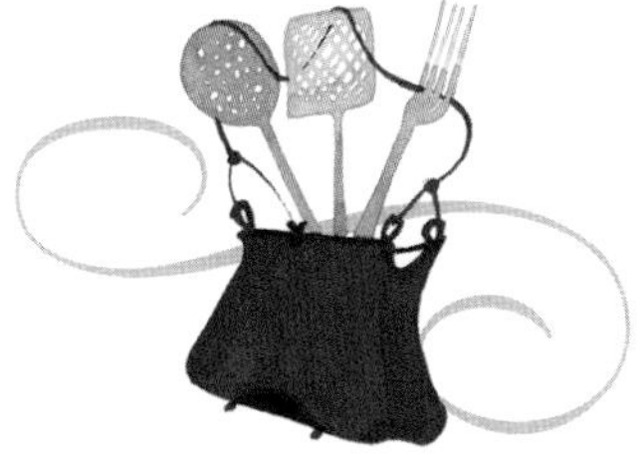

There, I guess King George will be able to read that.

JOHN HANCOCK, UPON SIGNING THE DECLARATION OF INDEPENDENCE

July 4, Independence Day! Such a relaxing holiday; I love the fact that you don't have to make elaborate plans in order to enjoy the Fourth. I always envision a Fourth of July picnic as a fifties montage of gingham checked shirts, pedal pushers with ballet flats, and a picnic basket filled to the brim with all the fixings for burgers on the grill, apple pie, potato chips, and soda (in an old-fashioned bottle with a straw). My reality has never matched the fantasy, but it's loads of fun to try for it.

On the Fourth of July, it's generally hot, hot, hot. You want to wear as little as possible. You also dream of making it through the cookout without a single stain (particularly if children are involved): less clothing, less to stain. So dress for fun and comfort. It's even OK to wear red, white, and blue—just do so with caution. Usually, I try to avoid a holiday color palette altogether, since wearing it can be cheesy; but red, white, and blue can look extremely chic if you do it right. Proportion is key; you want to avoid equal amounts of all three colors. Choose one foundation color and add touches of the other two. For instance, wear mostly blue with red and white accents.

What You Should Wear

ROMPER: An adorable romper is airy, comfortable, and the perfect blend of shorts and sundress.

BERMUDA SHORTS OR CAPRI PANTS IN A CRISP COTTON FABRIC: And no baggy Bermudas; only tailored, flattering ones! Spills are likely, so wear a medium to dark color or a print to be on the safe side. Full-on Americana.

SLEEVELESS TANK OR BUTTON-DOWN SHIRT: Cotton again, it's so breathable. Try it in a pretty red-and-white check or a plaid.

JACKET OR CARDIGAN: Bring something light to throw on after the sun goes down, while you're watching the fireworks.

ESPADRILLES: The pinnacle of casual, picnic chic, and they come in every height, from flat fisherman shoes to five-inch platform wedges.

ACCESSORIES: Bring a scarf for your hair in case the humidity takes over. Opt for simple jewelry; a chunky, wooden, or Bakelite bracelet is a perfect summer accessory.

THE coif THE face

Hair and makeup should be natural, of course. It's a little silly to vamp it up for a cookout, right? Sunscreen is an absolute must; mineral powder sunscreens are not pasty or greasy, don't cause blemishes, and do double duty as a foundation. They're an absolute revolution—and a revelation—in sun protection.

rule breakers we love

Marie Antoinette

Marie Antoinette was a true fashion icon in her time, both admired and reviled for refusing to follow court fashion etiquette. Unfortunately, while her excessive style was quite fabulous, it didn't go over well with the impoverished French citizens whose revolt led to her beheading. Sofia Coppola's film homage to Mme. Antoinette is a visual extravaganza of the infamous queen's lavish tastes.

EAT, DRINK, AND BE MERRY

A Red, White, and Blue Feast

- GUY FIERI'S FOURTH OF JULY COCKTAIL: 1 ounce watermelon schnapps, splash of cranberry juice, very thin slice of jalapeño, slice of lemon, slice of lime, 1½ ounces tequila, ¼ ounce blue curaçao, ½ ounce simple syrup. Scrumptious.
- RED, BLUE, AND FINGERLING POTATOES MIXED TOGETHER IN YOUR POTATO SALAD. You can also mix blue corn chips, sweet potato chips, and regular potato chips for a red, white, and blue effect.
- BOMB POPS: I don't eat popsicles often, but who can resist one on the Fourth of July?

Pure Style

What to Wear for Rosh Hashanah

Praying in the synagogue, hearing the shofar, festive meals with challah. Auspicious foods such as apples dipped in honey, fish heads and pomegranates, as well as new fruits on the second night. Refraining from work. What more can you ask from a holiday?

MICHAEL IAN BLACK

Rosh Hashanah is known as the Jewish New Year. However, unlike January 1, this is a religious holiday—no debauchery allowed. It is celebrated on the first day of Tishrei, the seventh month of the Hebrew calendar (corresponding roughly with September or October of the Gregorian calendar). This holiday celebrates the creation of the world and signals the start of ten days of judgment leading up to Yom Kippur, or the Day of Atonement.

Judaism views Rosh Hashanah as the start of the "high holidays," the time of year when one makes amends for past sins, appreciates loved ones, and begins anew. The look here is "dressy family conviviality." It is considered good luck to wear something new in honor of the New Year, and though your hosts won't know the difference, do you really need an excuse to wear something new? Splurge and make a debut on this occasion.

What You Should Wear

SEPARATES: As always, wear pants if you want to. Cut a striking figure with narrow men's style trousers or tuxedos and pair them with a belted sweater or a vest. A blouse with a high color, a ruffle or two, or French cuffs with cuff links rounds your look out beautifully. Think always fabulous Chanel.

DRESS: It's fall, so consider something with long sleeves, maybe a simple sheath or beautifully draped wool jersey. The palette should be relatively muted with subtle patterns if any, perhaps in a deep plum or dark gray.

COAT: Fall is perfect trench coat weather. Check out Alaïa's creations to fire up your imagination.

SHOES: Heels are welcome, or booties. Don't go stiletto, unless that's your thing, but a three-inch heel is just fine. Go flat with brogues or riding boots.

ACCESSORIES: Simple jewelry, a scarf, a classic watch.

NEW YEAR FARE

Symbol Meets Ritual

- APPLES AND HONEY: For a sweet New Year.
- DATES, BLACK-EYED PEAS, LEEKS, SPINACH, AND GOURD: All mentioned in the Talmud (the written text of Jewish law).
- MEAT FROM THE HEAD OF AN ANIMAL: Tongue, for instance, to signify the head (or start) of the year.
- CHALLAH: A round loaf of bread symbolizing the cycle of the year.
- POMEGRANATE SEEDS: A symbol of fertility and abundance. (Plus they're chock-full of nature's most potent antioxidants, so enjoy.)

Bone up on your Judaica, learn a few new customs (or refresh the old ones you've forgotten), and celebrate Rosh Hashanah with your unparalleled, and always spot-on, style. Mazel tov! (Congratulations!)

Costume Drama

What to Wear for Halloween

Secretly, I wanted to look like Jimi Hendrix, but I could never quite pull it off.

BRYAN FERRY

I'll just start off by confessing that I despise sexy cat costumes. With the exception of Halle Berry, I am equal parts annoyed and nervous every time I see a woman dressed up like an overgrown cat. Please hang up your been-there-done-that whiskers, tail, and fuzzy ears. Halloween is a time to really let go, have as much fun as you can, and, most of all, be creative. For the style mavens among us, Halloween is the ultimate game of dress up; a night stripped of regulation, where we can finally go completely Gaga (as in Lady) if we want to. So whip out your glue gun, get inspired, and go to town.

At the Office

Ah, Halloween at the office. It's 9 A.M., and the receptionist is dressed like a stabbing victim. Nice. By noon you've had so much candy corn you don't even want lunch. The very thought of Halloween in the workplace stirs a combination of fascination and dread. Most employees, frankly, don't want to see what their boss looks like in drag. And vice versa. Many offices don't expect or want their employees to dress up for Halloween (my personal preference). Don't get me wrong; I love Halloween and I love dressing up for it, just not at work. However, if you want to make a full day of costumes and trick or treat, it's best to plan a more toned down, office-friendly costume for the workday and save the real thing for after hours. Just, please, resist the urge to be a cat.

You don't necessarily have to come up with two completely different looks for work and for an evening bash—smart editing can do the trick. For some reason, many women like to dress up as a slutty fill-in-the-blank (slutty nurse, slutty policewoman, and so on) and many men enjoy the opportunity to dress as women (I'm not sure why, but it's interesting, no?). Neither of these options is suitable for the office. Even though you're in costume, nothing should detract from your ability to command respect from coworkers, subordinates, and bosses. Are you really going to walk your supervisor through that PowerPoint presentation dressed as a zombie? No, you are not. What you have on makes an impact on how others see you, even on Halloween.

> *Being in a band you can wear whatever you want— it's like an excuse for Halloween every day.*
>
> GWEN STEFANI

OFFICE HALLOWEEN PARTY *DON'TS*

- DON'T DRESS UP AS ANYONE IN THE OFFICE. Most people don't find mockery charming.
- DON'T WEAR A COSTUME THAT COULD BE PERCEIVED AS MAKING LIGHT OF A REAL TRAGEDY. No Charles Manson, Unabomber, or other notorious serial killer. Very bad taste.
- DON'T DRESS AS A POLITICAL OR RELIGIOUS FIGURE. You're virtually guaranteed to offend someone.
- DON'T WEAR ANYTHING THAT FULLY MASKS YOUR FACE. It's disconcerting in the workplace.
- DON'T DRESS AS A CLOWN. Many people are *really* scared of them, and you don't want your coworkers picturing you as a murderous clown for years to come.

OFFICE *DO'S*

- WEAR SOMETHING WITTY AND G-RATED.
- CHOOSE A COSTUME THAT IS NOT COMPLETELY CONTRARY TO YOUR NORMAL ATTIRE: nothing too wacky.
- USE YOUR IMAGINATION; be clever. Ingenuity reflects well on you.
- HAVE A BACKUP OUTFIT OF STREET CLOTHES in case no one else in the office is dressed up.

rule breakers we love

Björk

Yes, she was mocked unmercifully for wearing that swan dress to the 2001 Academy Awards, but you've got to admire her nerve. She committed to the look, right down to dropping an egg on the red carpet; she injected some much-needed inventiveness into the occasion. While everyone (well, almost everyone) looks terrific at award shows these days, I miss the pre-stylist era when the stars had to fend for themselves when dressing for the Oscars. There are far fewer missteps today, but it's not nearly as much fun to watch. Take note of Björk's fanciful approach to fashion when planning your Halloween costume, and in everyday life.

BEFORE LEAVING THE HOUSE, ASK YOURSELF:

- IS THIS TOO SEXY? The answer must be NO.
- WILL I BE EMBARRASSED TO SEE PICTURES OF MYSELF AROUND THE OFFICE WEARING IT? The answer must be NO.
- WOULD I WEAR THIS AROUND CHILDREN? The answer must be YES.

I always wanted to be Wonder Woman, of course. She had the greatest costume.

KELLY HU

I suggest a costume that doesn't require crazy makeup, revealing clothing, or bulky accoutrements. If you want to have fun with makeup, consider highlighting details, such as surrounding just one eye with a cool shade of glitter, or putting on a vibrant violet lip color. One Halloween, a good friend of mine, who happens to be a goldsmith, made herself two tiny, silver devil horns and attached them to her forehead, a look that was clever, sublimely understated, *and* chic. Another guest at that party went as a dish of candy; looking back, it is still one of my favorite costumes. She just wore a simple, black knit dress with penny candy sewed onto it. She accessorized with a candy necklace and bracelet. Fun, easy, and tasty.

If you're really ready to take it to the next level, come up with a costume that reflects where you would like to go in the company. A little subliminal advertising if you will. For instance, if you see yourself as the CEO someday, dress as Indra Nooyi (of PepsiCo); if you want to make partner or become a judge, dress as Supreme Court Justice Sonia Sotomayor. It can't hurt to put a powerful image in your boss's head. Wear a costume that impresses with your brilliance, not something that impresses with your lack of shame.

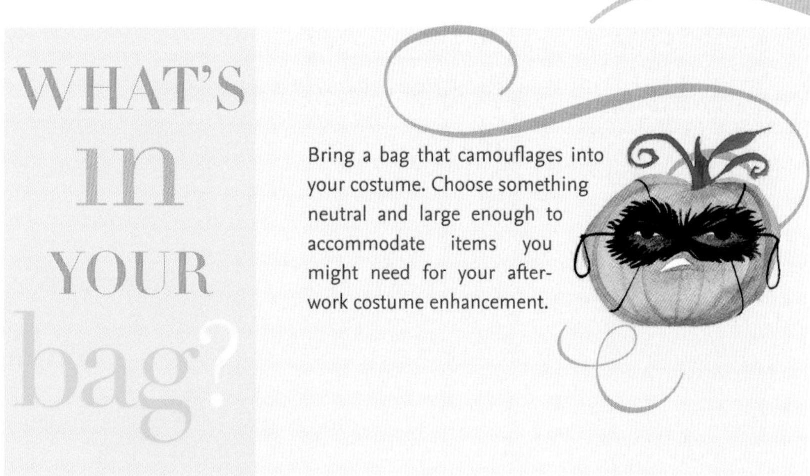

WHAT'S in YOUR bag?

Bring a bag that camouflages into your costume. Choose something neutral and large enough to accommodate items you might need for your after-work costume enhancement.

After Office Hours

An adult Halloween party allows you to let your freak flag fly. Everyone suppressing an inner slut and drag queen can let them run amok tonight. Often the best costumes are directly related to current events and pop culture, and thus are ever changing. Log on to PerezHilton.com and get inspired.

These Two Are Always a Crowd-Pleaser

- DEAD CELEBRITY: Live ones are popular too, but for some reason deceased celebrities are doubly popular.
- REALITY TV STAR: I don't know; for the most part I would say they are even too frightening for Halloween. Unless you're on *Project Runway*, in which case it's OK.

When you just don't want to spend a lot of time planning a costume, these oldies but goodies are still holding strong.

- Witch
- Vampire
- Pirate
- Nurse
- Athlete
- Cop

Go have fun, do take candy from strangers, and beware of masked men and zombies.

Autumnal Chic

What to Wear to Host Thanksgiving Dinner

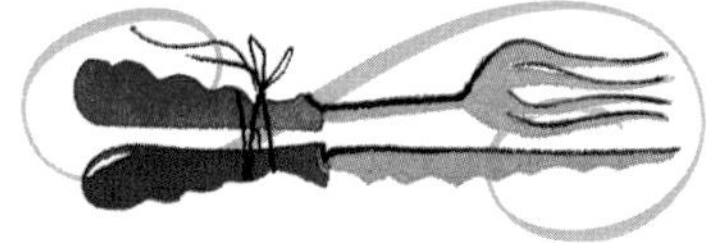

I don't believe in low-fat cooking.

NIGELLA LAWSON

Thanksgiving dinner is a wholly American holiday and despite being a total *colombiana*, I've embraced it with open arms. Hosting friends and family on this day is quite an undertaking, but it is a bit simpler than Christmas. And this is something to be thankful for! There's slightly less symbolic weight to Thanksgiving. It's not a religious holiday and you don't have to worry about presents; it's about reveling in food, drink, and company, and then RELAXING. The hard parts are cooking for so many guests and negotiating familial land mines.

We all have those land mines, and don't they add a splash of color to our lives? Well, maybe not, but they do keep us on our toes, and show us what this holiday is truly about: home and family, warts and all. Have a healthy sense of humor about it, and let your dress for the occasion reflect this.

My ultimate hostess attire for Thanksgiving dinner is slightly less dressy than what I wear at Christmas. I generally forgo platforms in favor of flats. Wide-leg trousers are always a go-to piece here, but in a nice wool or silk jersey rather than a dressier material. Pair the trousers with a cashmere sweater or turtleneck, and accessorize with simple jewelry; pearls or one or two gold lavalieres are perfection. Make it a little more *Annie Hall* than *Philadelphia Story*. This is an evening where you want to be at ease most of all.

BE PREPARED

- MAKE A LIST OF THINGS YOU ARE THANKFUL FOR. Keep it in your pocket and refer to it if something on the stove has boiled over, or the turkey didn't cook, or your uncle starts telling one of his endless stories. Study your list, take a deep breath, and soldier on.
- HAVE BOARD GAMES AND CARDS ON HAND to occupy restless guests if dinner takes longer than expected.
- SPRITZ YOURSELF WITH EVIAN FACIAL SPRAY if you're beginning to wilt. It will instantly revive you.
- DECORATE WITH FRESH FLOWERS in addition to the seasonal gourds. A beautiful table enhances your beauty.
- BUY A PACK OF ADJUST-A-BUTTONS. Whoever came up with these is a genius. You can instantly give yourself an extra inch of room in your waistband.

There's just no better accessory than a gorgeous apron to perfectly accent your hostess ensemble. And definitely leave room in your outfit for expansion. I can't think of a single traditional Thanksgiving food that isn't extremely filling. Surrender to the beginning of the holiday season and indulge yourself.

rule breakers we love

Babe Paley

Babe Paley was *the* glamorous hostess in mid-century New York café society. She was famous for her spectacular parties, wonderful people skills, breathtaking good looks, and unparalleled fashion sense. Add incredible wealth to these ingredients, and you have a true style icon.

MACY'S THANKSGIVING DAY PARADE

It's not just an iconic department store

- The first Macy's parade was actually a Christmas Parade in 1924. The following year it became the now famous Thanksgiving Day Parade.
- The Snoopy balloon has appeared more times than any other throughout the history of the parade.
- In 1927, the first year that helium balloons appeared in the parade, they were released above Manhattan and promptly exploded.
- The parade was first nationally televised in 1947; it has won nine Emmys, and over 44 million people watch it on television annually, while over 3 million see it in person each year.

After eating until I'm ready to burst, after the older guests have gone home, and once my son is fast asleep, I have my own little ritual—my husband and I make cocoa or hot toddies (so scrumptious) and settle in with my remaining guests to watch *Home for the Holidays*. We never get tired of it; Holly Hunter's family is phenomenally dysfunctional and I love it every time.

Talking Turkey

What to Wear for Thanksgiving with Your In-Laws (or Boyfriend's Family)

Your Thanksgiving hostess look doesn't need many alterations if you're going to brave dinner at the home of your in-laws. But there are subtle differences. Glam it up or tone it down as you see fit, and be happy that you're not the one charged with cooking and coordinating the entire meal. Use your freedom from cooking responsibility as an excuse to wear something that you really love. Carefully select the perfect outfit for eating, drinking, and being merry; lay it out on the bed; take a long, luxurious shower, then go charm the pants off them like only you can.

May your stuffing be tasty
May your turkey plump,
May your potatoes and gravy
Have nary a lump.
May your yams be delicious
And your pies take the prize,
And may your Thanksgiving dinner
Stay off your thighs!

ANONYMOUS

THANKSGIVING GUEST *DO'S*

- BRING A GIFT: a good bottle of wine, fresh flowers, or spicy scented candles. A gift is thoughtful and polite and starts everything off on a good note.
- OFFER TO BRING A DISH and, if they say no, stick to bringing wine or a dessert item. Some people are very particular about the menu but will feel obligated to serve your dish if you do bring one, while resenting the disruption. Wine is safe and always appreciated.
- OFFER TO HELP WITH THE COOKING and bring your apron! But back off if the in-laws say no.
- HELP CLEAR THE TABLE. You can be a little more insistent with this one, but if it looks like it's escalating into an argument, sit back and relax.
- COMPLIMENT THE MEAL A LOT, but don't come across as insincere.
- SEND A THANK-YOU NOTE (HANDWRITTEN, NOT AN EMAIL) WITHIN THREE DAYS. They'll love you for it.

GRATITUDE GARB *DON'TS*

- DON'T WEAR ANYTHING TOO TIGHT OR REVEALING. It's a family occasion and you don't want to be ogled by extended family, right? This dinner is similar to the first time you meet your boyfriend's parents. Reread that chapter. Same concepts apply.
- DON'T MOCK YOUR SIGNIFICANT OTHER'S DECORATING OR COOKING ABILITIES as a way of bonding with the other women at the table. It's not cute.
- DON'T DRINK TOO MUCH, for obvious reasons.
- DON'T DRINK TOO LITTLE; it's still a celebration.
- DON'T REFUSE SECONDS IF YOU WANT THEM. The cook will be so flattered; you can start your diet tomorrow.

Be yourself and take the time to chat and get to know your man's friends and family. You have the good fortune of being able to take a step back from the family drama; use this advantage to become a calming and uniting influence. Regardless of whether these people will be a part of your life forever, today you have a rare opportunity to bond with them and begin to appreciate what they mean to the man (or woman) you love. Jump in with both feet and you'll always have a fantastic Thanksgiving memory.

Gelt Glamour

What to Wear for Hanukkah

I'm a little different. My dreidel spins the other way.

ADAM LAMBERT

Hanukkah is actually not one of the more elaborately celebrated Jewish holidays, so don't expect a huge extravaganza at a Hanukkah dinner. Naturally, your hosts will be impressed by your terrific style, but if you can show that you understand what Hanukkah represents, it will kick their opinion of you up a notch. Most non-Jews are aware only that this holiday is celebrated around Christmastime, that a menorah is involved, and that it lasts for eight days. You've got to go deeper than that.

So before you even think about what to wear, here's a little Hanukkah 101.

The Miracle

The holiday begins at sunset on the twenty-fifth day of Kislev (a month in the Hebrew calendar, which corresponds roughly to November or December of the Gregorian calendar), and lasts until sunset eight days later. Hanukkah commemorates the rededication of the Holy Temple in Jerusalem after the Jews seized it back from the Syrians, in the second century B.C. The Temple's sacred lamp holding the eternal flame had only enough consecrated olive oil to burn for one day, but, miraculously, the flame lasted for eight days.

To celebrate this wonder, Jews light a ceremonial candelabra called a menorah. Each night of the holiday, one candle is used to light the others:

one on the first night, two on the second, and so on until all nine candles are burning on the eighth night.

> *Just as a candle cannot burn without fire,*
> *men cannot live without a spiritual life.*
>
> BUDDHA

What You'll Do and What You'll Eat

Before a meal during Hanukkah, the menorah is lit and children are given a small gift and some gelt (foil-wrapped chocolate coins—reason alone to want to convert). You might sing a song or two before the children play the dreidel game. It's a lovely, cozy holiday. And there's an emphasis on delicious food—potato pancakes fried in olive oil, called latkes, and special doughnuts called *sufganiot*, which is the Hebrew word for, well, doughnuts.

Best Looks for Latkes

Dress up a little but don't go crazy. Hanukkah is generally not an incredibly formal dinner. It's usually a nice jeans or pretty winter dress kind of affair. The look is "traditional family celebration." Think simple, clean lines and cozy fabrics. Emphasize texture over color.

rule breakers we love

Barbara Walters

In 1974 Barbara Walters became the first woman to coanchor an evening news program. She's one of the first beautiful women to be taken seriously in the male-dominated world of TV news. The press has ribbed her about adopting the style of whatever celebrity she's interviewing—poke fun if you will, but it's clear Ms. Walters knows a little something about dressing to put others at ease.

What You Should Wear

SEPARATES: A pretty wool dress or skirt is always welcome. Something simple with exquisite detailing in an A-line cut and a modest, just-below-the-knee hem would do very nicely. Match it with an easy sweater, maybe a wraparound style with a T-shirt underneath. Or, if you opt to wear pants, choose a nice pair of high-waisted wool trousers with an unusual cut, perhaps narrow legs or a paper bag waist. Top it off with a simple jacket or blazer and you have the perfect outfit for a traditional family celebration.

COAT: You'll probably need a warm winter coat. Continue with the wool theme, or perhaps go to an always-stylish camel-colored coat. Something by Smythe, for example.

SHOES: Dressy but not too much. Booties or pumps or spiffy brogues should do it.

ACCESSORIES: Keep it simple; a pendant and a cuff, or some large hoop earrings. Finally, set your look off with a beautiful belt.

GIFTS FOR THE HOSTESS

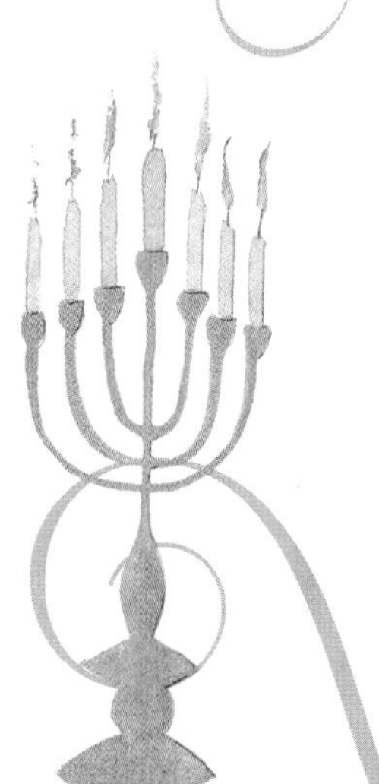

Worried about bringing an appropriate hostess gift? It's so simple.

- A BOTTLE OF WINE IS ALWAYS APPRECIATED. Look for a kosher wine. Even if the family does not maintain a kosher kitchen, it's best to err on the side of tradition.
- A REALLY NICE BOTTLE OF ISRAELI OLIVE OIL IS A FABULOUSLY THOUGHTFUL HANUKKAH GIFT. The Tishbi winery in Benyamina, Israel, presses a delectable olive oil, and they ship worldwide.
- BRING A DELICIOUS TRADITIONAL DESSERT SUCH AS RUGELACH.
- AND DON'T FORGET TO BRING SOME CHOCOLATE GELT FOR THE KIDS.

Santa Baby

What to Wear When You're Hosting Christmas

Christmas, children, is not a date.
It is a state of mind.

MARY ELLEN CHASE

There's something about Christmas that tugs at the core of my heart. It brings memories of my sister and me as children, and of the elaborate antics my parents would pull in order to hide Santa's gifts from us. They told us about trips to Santa's workshop and about their conversations with him. Had we been good enough during the year to be worthy of the gifts on our wish list? When Christmas Eve arrived, we waited until midnight, when we were finally allowed to tackle the presents under our tree, then we woke early the next morning to find what Santa had brought. The smiles and the love, the ribbons and wrapping paper, even the smell of the cookies my mother had baked the day before, still wafting through the air, are some of my most vivid memories.

I still adore the holiday decorations, the snow that may fall (if we're lucky), hot cocoa, and the feeling of festive anticipation. Luckily for me, absolutely nothing compares to the lights and window displays in New York City at this time of year, and I still look forward to them as November approaches.

Yes, it's Christmas. Time to turn up that *Bing Crosby Sings Christmas Songs* CD and roll with the spirit.

rule breakers we love

Martha Stewart

Martha is the ultimate hostess. No one will ever match her ability to cook a perfect dinner, set a perfect table, and maintain her composure in a classically tasteful way.

Remember that the fashion-forward mind never lives in the past. One must create new memories, and maybe even a new tradition or two. My personal favorite: the guava martini. We tried it one year and now it's a custom—and a lovely way to bring a touch of the tropics to what is usually a frosty time. Hosting Christmas dinner for your family and friends is a rite of passage into adulthood. Once you've made it through this marathon holiday meal unscathed, it's official, you're a grown-up. But the meal *is* a marathon. As wonderful as Christmas is, and as much as you love your family, this is an all-day affair complete with overexcited children on sugar highs and all of the emotional button-pushing that only your nearest and dearest can do so skillfully. Keep plenty of wine on hand; you'll need it. You'll also need an impeccable, comfortable ensemble.

The dress must not hang on the body but follow its lines. It must accompany its wearer and when a woman smiles the dress must smile with her.

MADELEINE VIONNET

GLOBAL FARE

Christmas Dishes Served Around the World

- COLOMBIA: Natilla (a dessert of milk, corn starch, and cinnamon) and buñuelos (cheese fritters). My favorites, of course.
- ENGLAND: The infamous Christmas pudding, a heavy, black steamed pudding made with fruit and nuts. Very close to the American version of a fruitcake.
- FRANCE: Bûche de Noël, or Yule log, consisting of a sponge cake rolled with a layer of filling, and decorated to look like a log. Scrumptious.
- ITALY: Panettone, a round loaf of bread, deliciously fluffy and sweet.
- GERMANY: Stollen, another fruitcake variation.
- LEBANON: Tabbouleh, kibbeh, and turkey.
- PHILIPPINES: Queso de Bola, or cheese ball, tsokolate (hot chocolate), and ham.

Festive attire is a must. After all, isn't dressing up for Christmas dinner half the fun? And I am NOT talking about sweaters festooned with reindeer or snowflake appliqués. I *am* talking about holiday chic. An outfit that will hold up through cooking, eating, *and* exchanging gifts, a look that is functional as well as fabulous.

Christmas dinner is the occasion for opulent fabrics like velvet, brocade, or my personal favorite: cashmere. Think cozy/luxe. And bear in mind that there will be copious numbers of photos. Your ensemble will show up on mantelpieces and in photo albums for years to come, so you've got to be picture perfect (although, if you're camera shy, hostess duties are an excellent excuse for ducking out of photo ops).

What You Should Wear

To play the part of the consummate Christmas hostess, envision Katharine Hepburn in *Philadelphia Story*. She was beautiful, independent, and she had to do a lot of running around in great outfits. The forties produced some fabulous silhouettes that still influence today's designers.

DRESS: If you feel more "done" in a dress, pick one that's body skimming but not too tight. Christmas is a time for eating and drinking without obsessing about your waistline. Choose something that has a fitted waist and a full or draped skirt, with a hem that hits just below the knee. This cut is flattering on almost everyone, and you'll be able to sit without worrying about giving any children who are camped out on the living room floor playing with their Christmas haul a show.

TROUSERS: Perfectly tailored, wide-leg trousers in a sumptuous fabric like velvet or silk. I prefer trousers to dresses when hosting, because wearing them makes me feel like I'm ready to spring into action as hostess at a moment's notice.

BLOUSE: An extravagant blouse with a fitted bodice and voluminous sleeves, a high collar and French cuffs (then you can accessorize with gorgeous cuff links—so unusual and fun). I love the look of a sheer blouse over a camisole, but if that's too daring for a family dinner, a more modest but still luxurious fabric such as silk or fine cotton will do.

COAT: December means you need to bundle up. Julie Christie and Geraldine Chaplin epitomize winter chic in *Dr. Zhivago*.

SHOES: Platform pumps. Not too sexy but super chic and pretty. Or go for a pair of elegant flats, both functional and formal.

ACCESSORIES: Keep it simple and be mindful of what dishes you'll be cooking and serving. There's nothing appetizing about a diamond pendant (real or faux) taking a dip in the gravy on its way to the table. Chandelier earrings or a necklace will add that extra bit of oomph. Christmas is a sentimental time, so bring out your heirloom pearls or cameo. Wear a watch—you don't want anything overcooked—and don't forget the cuff links.

Be Your Own Photo Editor

If you have one of those candid-shot enthusiasts on the guest list, familiarize yourself with various cameras ahead of time. Then just ask to see the photos before he or she leaves, and quickly "accidentally" delete any that that you don't consider flattering. This may seem a tad extreme, but sometimes you just have to go there.

THE coif THE face

The last thing you want to worry about when hosting a holiday dinner party is maintaining your hair and makeup. Opt for a simple ponytail or updo and very natural makeup. Red lipstick looks better in photos, but it's preferable to go for a nude lip than be caught with the dreaded outline effect, so be realistic about how much upkeep your lips will require.

The Modern Apron

I am a huge fan of the flouncy apron for protecting your ensemble while cooking. A fantastic apron gives a woman that instant domestic diva vibe and puts the exclamation point on every holiday party. If frilly isn't your taste (and I totally hear that), go for something simple but festive that enhances what you are wearing. The apron is a truly underrated and enormously useful accessory. Any woman who plans to host many dinners must have *at least* one or two gorgeous, company-ready aprons.

CHRISTMAS CLOTHING *DON'TS*

- DON'T WEAR THE HIDEOUS CHRISTMAS SWEATER your in-laws or your aunt gave you last year. While you may wish to be polite, wearing said sweater will only encourage them to buy you many more just like it. Life's too short, and closet space too valuable.
- DON'T WEAR ANYTHING TOO SHORT OR LOW CUT. This is a family occasion.
- DON'T WORRY ABOUT OVERDRESSING. The hostess is never overdressed.
- DON'T WEAR RED AND GREEN. I don't think I need to elaborate on this one. The bottom line is that you do not want to look like you have just stepped off the set of the film *Elf*.

Your comfortably fierce ensemble will set the tone for the day as you greet your guests calmly and cheerfully, surrounded by friends and family for a day of eating, drinking, and truly being merry.

Dare to Dazzle

What to Wear for Christmas with the In-Laws (or Boyfriend's Family)

Of all the peoples whom I have studied,
from city dwellers to cliff dwellers,
I always find at least 50 percent
would prefer to have at least one jungle
between themselves and their mother-in-law.

MARGARET MEAD

Celebrating Christmas at the home of your in-laws, or significant other's parents, relieves you of hostess stress (which counts for a lot), but it comes with its own special issues. This gathering is an event that will likely go on for hours, so most of my suggestions for hostess dress apply here as well. Think functional formality. On the plus side, attending this soiree is the equivalent of a 5K run, as opposed to the 10K run that is hosting your own Christmas party. The downside is that you don't know everyone on the guest list, so there's a wild card factor; and you may not know beforehand just how extravagant the fete is or is not going to be—especially if you're meeting the in-laws for the first time, which is often the case during the holidays.

Beyond looking fantastic, my best advice for holidays with the in-laws is to be punctual, be accommodating, and remain calm no matter what. And don't take anything that happens too personally. Holidays bring out the best *and* the worst in people.

Do your best to get as much advance info as you can; at the very least find out how formal the dinner will be. Men can be shockingly inarticulate about this sort of thing; see if you can get your guy to show you pictures of holidays past. If you have met his parents before, you already have a good idea of what you're dealing with, but one can never be too careful. Many people get hostess stress during Christmas, and this may affect the mood of the party, which in turn will affect how you should dress.

Essentially, wear something similar to what I described for hosting Christmas dinner, but think about slightly toning down the look—you never want to upstage the mother-in-law. A matriarch on Christmas needs to glow; honor that. It's also not a bad idea to bring an apron along, just in case you wind up helping with dinner. Your mother-in-law will adore you for this, and further welcome you to the family. You want to look very nice (a little better than very nice, really), but never better than the hostess.

Keep your hair and makeup simple, perhaps a smooth chignon or low ponytail. Pink or peachy lips are friendlier and easier to maintain than deep scarlet. Go easy on the blush; there will likely be lots of conviviality, so you will attain a natural glow as the evening wears on. Dazzle his family with your natural beauty and effervescence and they'll welcome you with open arms.

Your outfit should say: I respect you and your home, and I'm a fabulous, practical woman who is perfect for your son. Your outfit should feel comfortable and reassuring. In order to maintain an easy grace throughout the day, you must be able to move, and put any thoughts of wardrobe malfunctions out of your mind.

If your in-laws are very informal and prefer low-key basics like jeans, T-shirts, and cozy sweaters for the holidays, you should adjust accordingly. If you show up dressed for fabulosity, and everyone else is in sweatshirt mode, they'll feel slighted, you'll be self-conscious, and no one wants that. Never wear anything that you wouldn't normally put on—this is not an audition; always be true to yourself while acknowledging the occasion's context. Wear something that *you* feel good in.

> *I stopped believing in Santa Claus when I was six. Mother took me to see him in a department store and he asked for my autograph.*
>
> SHIRLEY TEMPLE

WHAT'S in YOUR bag?

Throw in a camera to record the memories, and a little touch-up kit to keep your makeup fresh. Blotting paper is a lifesaver. You might bring little trinkets or gifts for the hostess, such as cute Christmas ornaments or a delicious scented candle.

life
events

Special Delivery

How to Pack a Hospital Bag for Your Baby's Birth

I'm three times the girl I used to be.

HALLE BERRY

Fine. So you've taken to eating fried chicken and caramel popcorn for dinner, your ankles have totally disappeared, and you've gone up three cup sizes (exciting, yes, but also a bit daunting). You're eight months pregnant and you feel like you're ready to burst. Despite these rather overwhelming physical changes, the arrival of your first baby is one of the most thrilling experiences a woman will go through. Of course, if you're anything like the rest of womankind, you're reaching the point where you're completely sick of being pregnant and getting nervous about how you'll make it through labor and delivery. So it's time to pack your maternity bag. You're in the home stretch, and you have to (at least try to) be ready when the moment hits.

Never underestimate the value of a well-packed maternity bag. It can provide an island of tranquility, carrying you gently through the chaos of labor, new baby joy, visitors, and pictures galore. Foresight is key here.

Very soon, you won't be able to even think about what you bring to the maternity ward; all you'll care about is leaving the hospital 8 to 10 pounds lighter, carrying your healthy baby in your arms. So dry your eyes now and take a deep breath, because you can make it through this journey—looking totally gorgeous.

One of the perks of being stuck in a hospital bed is that you only need to look good from the waist up. From the waist down it's all about comfort. Pamper yourself by indulging in a soft, cozy bed jacket with a sweet satin sash. The retro fifties vibe will put you in the consummate Donna Reed frame of mind for your new role as a perfect Mom. Think January Jones in *Mad Men*. When you get home, you'll be pretty as a picture, lounging on a lazy Sunday, waiting for your husband to bring you breakfast in bed—I promise, you *will* have lazy Sundays again . . . in a few years.

> *I'm not interested in being Wonder Woman in the delivery room. Give me drugs.*
>
> MADONNA

PACKING LIST

Here is a no-fail list of necessities for your trip to the hospital.

- NIGHTIES (OR PAJAMAS)
- BED JACKET
- CHANGE OF CLOTHES TO WEAR HOME
- MAKEUP: You don't need the full arsenal here, just the basics.
- TOOTHBRUSH, TOOTHPASTE
- HAIRBRUSH
- SLIPPERS
- FLIP-FLOPS
- BATHROBE
- ID
- BIRTHING PLAN/MEDICAL INFO
- GLASSES/CONTACTS AND SOLUTION

- MATERNITY UNDERWEAR, SEVERAL PAIRS
- SNACKS FOR VISITORS: You can still be a great hostess from your hospital bed. Pack something easy and pre-packaged like little bags of pretzels, crackers, or cookies. Miniature boxes of chocolates are always appreciated.

You will want entertainment. Bring magazines, your trusted baby books (for last-minute prep), and an iPod full of relaxing music (lots of it). You might want to personalize your hospital room a bit, so you can truly relax. Bring framed photographs of people you love or prop up a picture of your pets; do whatever you can to make the room an inviting, happy place for you.

A brush, a comb, and a touch of hair product are a must. Just enough to pull those tresses back and smooth down the flyaways. In case you're not up to tackling your coif right away, you might defer to a flattering scarf. Remember, the neater the better.

As for makeup, believe me, you're going to want it. You won't be taking glamour shots in the maternity ward, so just pack the basics. A touch of mascara, powder, concealer, blush, and lip gloss are all you'll need to look naturally camera ready.

What You Should Wear

NIGHTIE: Bring a few nighties; you'll want a couple of changes. Pajamas work too, but nighties are much easier to get in and out of. If you want to go all out for this event, buy a delivery gown or two.

BED JACKET: A pretty, luxurious, satiny jacket to throw on when visitors come. A shawl or cardigan is also a welcome option. Anything to cozy up your look and lessen the icy, clinical vibe of the hospital.

ROBE: Something roomy that will keep you adequately covered for those treks down the hall. Look for fluffy, touchable fabrics like chenille or flannel; pockets are always helpful.

DRESS: A fresh ensemble for the ride home. Choose something easy and comfortable like a long cotton sweater dress or a tunic over leggings. You and your baby will arrive home in total style. Get ideas from Heidi Klum's Loved and Lavish maternity collections or Christian Siriano's Fierce Mamas.

FLUFFY SLIPPERS: If you can avoid touching anything in the hospital with your bare skin, you should, *especially* the floor. And don't forget flip-flops for the shower. Hospitals are crawling with germs, so do what you can to stay protected.

rule breakers we love

M.I.A.

M.I.A. performed at the 2009 Grammys in a sheer minidress, just days before giving birth. Yes, the voluminous blue gown she wore on the red carpet was a tad too much, but she made an unforgettable statement: Pregnancy doesn't have to hold women back from anything, in fashion or life.

THE 411

Q. Who's likely to visit?

A. Everyone you know, especially if it's your first baby.

Q. How long will I be staying?

A. Probably just a day or two, but prepare for three.

Q. Am I going to be videotaped?

A. That is entirely up to you.

Q. Will I be photographed?

A. Definitely and copiously.

Q. Do I want to look pretty?

A. Of course you do. Everyone's entranced with the baby, but there's no reason you shouldn't be a beautiful, glowing Madonna.

Who's Your Daddy?

What to Wear to Meet a Potential Surrogate

It is not the strongest of the species that survive,
nor the most intelligent,
but the ones most responsive to change.

CHARLES DARWIN

When nature throws us a curveball, we women know how to get the job done. And you're no exception. Once you've made the difficult decision to enlist the help of a surrogate to carry your child, you have to begin the even more difficult task of finding the perfect woman. And, of course, when you do find her and you're meeting her for the first time, you need the perfect outfit to wear. Don't try to deny it; you know you're going to be checking her out, looking for signs of wisdom in the skirt she's chosen, or evidence of emotional stability in her footwear. It's certain she'll be doing the same with you—it's a feminine reflex. So let's use the unspoken language of fashion to get you properly dressed for this critical meeting.

You and your surrogate will share a unique bond based on trust and very, very clear boundaries, so what exactly do you want this ensemble to say? You want it to communicate: "I'm an excellent mother," "I'm a good person," "You won't have even a split second of doubt about trusting me with the baby that you've been carrying for nine months."

This look is a tall order. You've got to come up with an ensemble fit for a job interview, but mixed with a first date. Something that won't intimidate or put off your potential surrogate and will instead express that this could be the beginning of a wonderful partnership.

You're aiming for a relaxed air of reassurance combined with a clear air of self-assurance. Luckily, there are excellent style role models for this. Joan Lunden has two sets of twins, and Sarah Jessica Parker has one set that were conceived with the aid of a surrogate. These ladies both know how to put together a phenomenal look with their eyes closed. So when in doubt, refer to Joan and SJP.

Again, Sarah Jessica Parker truly is the epitome of how to look like a million bucks yet remain totally approachable. She always looks like she's having a blast. Wouldn't you love to meet her for coffee to chat? Emulate her down-to-earth style with the ensemble you wear to meet your potential surrogate.

> *Always end the name of your child with a vowel, so that when you yell, the name will carry.*
>
> BILL COSBY

What You Should Wear

SEPARATES: Chic cargo pants in olive or a toasty brown color, or carrot pants in navy blue. A casual but neat oxford style shirt over a tank or tee is pulled together without appearing stuffy. You want to look neat and organized, but never uptight. A pretty dress or skirt is a perfectly good option as well. Prints and color are always welcome, but stay away from anything too loud or busy. The focus is on you for this occasion.

JACKET: A short, fitted blazer or an oversize cashmere cardigan in a muted hue. Warm gray or camel look fantastic with just about everything.

SHOES: Brogues or ballet flats. Whatever you feel most at ease in. Perhaps a comfortably worn-in pair of relaxed boots along the lines of Frye would do the trick.

ACCESSORIES: A simple watch is the perfect accessory; it conveys punctuality and responsibility. A signet ring and chunky stud earrings add just the right finishing touches. Don't overdo it with the jewelry; the emphasis should be on your personality. A lovely scarf will finish your look very nicely.
BAG: Wear a practical shoulder bag, without logos, that's not too large or bulky.

rule breakers we love

Sarah Jessica Parker

Sarah Jessica Parker enlisted the help of a surrogate and had a great experience. When it comes to fashion, she has her own unique style separate and apart from her alter ego, Carrie Bradshaw. It's clear that she is a woman who really has fun with fashion and appreciates a beautifully made gown.

CELEBS WITH SURROGATES

You're in good company. These are just a few of the amazing women who have chosen the surrogacy route.

- JOAN LUNDEN: She did it twice and wrote a book about it.
- MARISSA JARET WINOKUR: After surviving cervical cancer, she went this route.
- KELLY KLEIN: She didn't let being divorced and already fifty years old stop her from having a baby.
- TAYLOR DAYNE: Wanted one baby, got two, couldn't be happier.
- SARAH JESSICA PARKER: She wanted her son to have a sibling, and now he has two!

Because I am a mother,
I am capable of being shocked;
as I never was when I was not one.

MARGARET ATWOOD

As you prepare for this meeting, remind yourself that you are an amazing woman and a fabulous judge of character. Your personality is a major asset and your impeccably casual ensemble communicates your self-possession, sincerity, and kindness (as well as your deft fashion sense). The two of you will come to the right decision about whether this is the right surrogacy match. And if it isn't, be patient; your perfect surrogate is out there and you'll find her. Then you can go shopping and help her pick out maternity clothes. Fun!

WHAT'S in YOUR bag?

Family photos to share with your potential surrogate (you've got to get to know each other), tissues (it's emotional), and a notebook (to keep the facts straight).

Sweet Chic

What to Wear to a Baby Shower

Every child begins the world again.

HENRY DAVID THOREAU

I have never been to an unpleasant baby shower! It's such an inherently joyful event. No one ever drinks too much, there's no drama; this party is all about girl talk, snacks, gifts, and baby bliss. The expectant mother is aglow and surging with pre-birth adrenalin. You and her other friends have been watching her expanding belly with a combination of excitement, delight, and disbelief. I remember when the first of my friends got pregnant—it was such a thrilling moment. Even more than getting married, your first child means you are not only an adult, you are a *mom*.

rules are made to be broken

A pregnant woman should dress to conceal her belly.

Just the opposite. When you're voluminous, adding even more volume only makes you look larger. Enhance your new curves with body-conscious clothing that stretches to accommodate your shape. No maternity tents, ladies.

> *If men had to have babies,*
> *they would only ever have one each.*
>
> PRINCESS DIANA

These parties are usually semi-casual affairs. What woman in her third trimester wants to deal with dressing up? Go easy on the glam. The idea is to keep it fun and feminine. Although my esteemed colleague Heidi Klum and many other fabulous women (Gwyneth Paltrow, Amy Adams, Camila Alves, and Cate Blanchett come to mind) look fantastic on the red carpet with their baby bumps proudly displayed and fabulously adorned.

Of course, gifts are the best part of a baby shower. It's impossible not to love baby things. If it isn't an adorable miniature version of a grown-up item, it's a quirky or nostalgic toy, or a stupefying piece of baby gadgetry. A fascinating variety and quantity of contraptions accompany the birth of an infant. Your first baby shower is not just a celebration; it's an education.

GIFT IDEAS

- *PAT THE BUNNY:* Or any absolute favorite baby book of yours. I remember playing with *Pat the Bunny* as a child.
- SOMETHING FOR MOM: She's going to be overloaded with baby paraphernalia, and pregnancy's not easy. Give her a luxurious bath or lotion set. A pregnant woman can never have too much pampering or too much lotion.
- SOMETHING FOR DAD: Add a little something extra for Dad; if Mom's feeling overshadowed by baby things, he's eclipsed.
- A FLOWERING PLANT: A plant symbolizes new life and growth, perfect for a new baby.
- AN IOU FOR MEALS: Give her a week's worth of meals when she brings the baby home. She is NOT going to want to cook.

Now back to your look. Baby showers involve a lot of sitting and standing and passing around gifts, and helping to keep the wrapping paper from taking over the room. This is also one of life's many well-photographed events; bear that in mind when you're getting dressed. These days, photos don't just show up in albums for years to come. Facebook is the paparazzi of the non-celebrity. Before you know it, the picture of you with a mouthful of food, wearing a pair of regrettable pants, is on your friend's wall, and she's tagged it so that everyone you went to high school with is alerted to its presence. Yikes. So mind your angles, girls. And come up with an outfit that will be fit for showering the new mom with gifts and love.

What You Should Wear

JEANS: Easy denim that you can move in is a simple choice. Boot cut and dark rinse if you're feeling uptown, skinny and distressed if you're in a downtown, boho mood.

TROUSERS: An awful lot of babies are born in the summer (all that winter snuggling). So if it's too warm for jeans, go for loose cotton pants or slim shorts. A summer dress or a romper is also ideal for a baby shower. Choose a colorful palette; this is a celebration, so cheerful hues are perfect. Etro features clothes in absolutely beautiful floral prints.

TOP: A sweet scalloped shirt (short- or long-sleeved; compromise with three-quarter length), or a gauzy tunic over skinny jeans or leggings. A button-down shirt always looks smart with a pair of narrow pants or jeans.

SHOES: Sandals, either flat thongs or pretty wedges.

ACCESSORIES: A charm bracelet that jingles when you pass around the gifts to ooh and aah. Colorful earrings. Perhaps a belt or scarf with a little character.

Sip iced tea, reminisce about your college days, complain about the men in your life, and eat scrumptious little canapés—all while exchanging baby advice and enjoying a lovely afternoon. You may not be seeing the new mom this relaxed again for quite a while, so give her a fabulous baby shower that will gently nudge and support her toward her big day.

Baby Bliss

What to Wear to a Baby Ceremony

My mother says I didn't open my eyes for eight days after I was born, but when I did, the first thing I saw was an engagement ring. I was hooked.

ELIZABETH TAYLOR

Two questions that I'm asked a lot are: "What should I wear to a bris?" and "What should I wear to a christening/baptism?" Fortunately, you can wear pretty much the same outfit to both.

A B'rith Milah, or bris, is the ritual circumcision of a Jewish boy that takes place eight days after his birth. Usually only family members are invited to the actual circumcision (that's a load off). Traditionally, this event is not announced through conventional methods like printed invites; it's usually a word of mouth or email invite type of affair. After the ceremony, there is a big party, often involving bagels and smoked fish, to celebrate this rite of passage, which may take place at the temple or just at the parents' home.

You'll need an outfit that's adequate for church or temple and an afternoon party. Simple, right? You don't need your Sunday best: instead, think Sunday Chic. Geri Halliwell wore a blue sheath to her daughter Bluebell's christening, in honor of the baby's name; Elizabeth Hurley wore a low-cut number with fur to her son's christening; and Gwen Stefani wore a smart gray suit to her son's affair. I know these ladies aren't what you would call "typical," but they do illustrate the breadth of suitable attire.

Of course, you don't want to wear anything that's too bare—no plunging décolletage (Liz Hurley can pull it off, but she's Liz Hurley). It's a baby-driven event. (You don't want to tempt the guest of honor.) Also, skip the miniskirt, the jeans, and the sneakers; beyond those, you're pretty safe with whatever you choose.

What You Should Wear

SEPARATES: Trousers with a nice blouse can also be quite smart. Naturally, you will base your fabric choices on the season. Give your demure look an edge by choosing trousers with a paper-bag waist and cinching them with a unique belt.

DRESS: A demure dress with a knee-length hem is a great option. Keep it interesting with a touch of embellishment like ruffles, or contrasting collar and cuffs. Soft colors and floral prints are perfect for this occasion. Look to Moschino or Chloé for ladylike inspiration.

JACKET: A short jacket or fitted cardigan, also in a soft color.

COAT: You can never go wrong with a trench. And you can never go wrong with Burberry or Prada.

SHOES: Pumps or dainty sandals, if the weather is warm; if it's cold outside, booties or brogues.

ACCESSORIES: Throw on a light scarf. Keep the trimmings pared down; a string of pearls or a simple pendant always looks elegant. You don't need a lot of flash.

BAG: A small handbag is appropriate. Something basic and discreet.

A BRIEF HISTORY OF CHRISTENING GOWNS

- Christening gowns came into use in the seventeenth century. Originally infants were carried to their christening in a large, ornately embellished square of white silk called a bearing cloth.
- During the eighteenth century, the bearing cloth evolved into a dress that fastened in the front with ribbons. A slip dress with short sleeves and a long skirt was worn underneath.
- In the mid-nineteenth century, Scottish Ayrshire embroidery was a popular christening gown addition. Ayrshire is extremely intricate white embroidery.
- In the Victorian era, the gowns became even more decorative, with touches like pin tucks, lavish embroidery, lace inserts, and a matching bonnet.

> *I didn't know how babies were made until I was pregnant with my fourth child.*
>
> LORETTA LYNN

BRIS LINGO

MOHEL: A Jewish man trained in circumcision and the accompanying religious rituals. He's usually a doctor, a rabbi, or both.
KVATTER: The *Kvatter* or *Kvatterin* (female) among Ashkenazi Jews is the person who carries the baby from the mother to the father, who in turn carries him to the mohel. This honor is usually given to a couple without children, as a blessing for them to have children of their own.

Cool in School

What to Wear to a Parent/Teacher Meeting

The greatest sign of success for a teacher is to be able to say, "The children are now working as if I did not exist."

MARIA MONTESSORI

OK, this is important. (And it's not even style related!) Be a present parent, a parent who is always involved. Develop a relationship with your child's teachers. This will keep you in the loop and allow you to be a part of your child's day-to-day life outside of the home. A good parent/teacher relationship benefits everybody, but most importantly your child. And how you present yourself to your child's teachers does have an impact on how your child is perceived and treated at school. Come across as mature, responsible, and honest. If you want your kids to reflect well on you, shouldn't you do the same for them?

This is particularly important if you have a "spirited" youngster. You need to make sure the teacher(s) understand that you are serious about helping your child to improve his or her behavior. If you come into the meeting wearing spandex and smelling like cigarettes, the teacher might—even subconsciously—become less convinced of your child's chances for success. If the teacher is confident that there's serious backup at home, they will be more amenable to putting in a little extra work in the classroom.

Think of this as a business meeting. You're probably coming straight from work anyway. Don't go crazy. The power suit can stay in the closet. But plan your outfit with the same care you apply when you have a presentation at work. The look should say: "I'm a good person and an involved parent, and I'm open to your suggestions." Mutual respect is mandatory, as is a "Let's collaborate on making the best possible educational setting for my child" attitude.

THE coif THE face

Hair, smooth. Makeup, bare. Avoid bright colors and anything sloppy or flashy.

What You Should Wear

SEPARATES: Sensible and smart. Something simple, sophisticated, and crisp, with clean lines. No loud colors or patterns, and nothing froufrou. Go for low-key basics like J.Crew or Donna Karan.

JACKET: A blazer or jacket. No motorcycle or bomber jackets. Be a grown-up. (Even just this once.)

COAT: A trench—smart and chic.

SHOES: Pumps. You want the authoritative click of not-too-high heels down the corridor as you approach your child's classroom.

rule breakers we love

Taylor Momsen

Her style is the quintessential rebellious teen. Too much eyeliner, too much lipstick, visible garters, torn stockings . . . I'd probably lock her in her room if I were her mother, but as a detached observer, I admire that she owns her look. Emulate her spirit and rebellious nature—not necessarily her fashion sense.

If you've been called to the principal's office because your kid did something wrong, take the seriousness factor up a notch, look that principal in the eye, and promise that you'll take charge of the situation. Try to kill the teacher with kindness, while remembering that you were a kid once too.

Just Do It

What to Wear to Your Child's Sporting Event/Play

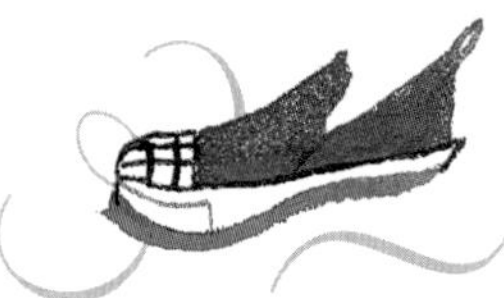

I've had enough tennis for the week. I'm still in school so I'm going to relax by doing economics.

MARIA SHARAPOVA

Remember school plays and field hockey games? I wasn't much of an actress or an athlete, but I dabbled in both and loved running around on the soccer field with my friends. I always wanted my parents to come see me and be proud of my performance. But I also wanted them to pretend they didn't know me in front of the other kids. Oh, the joys of being a parent. I'm excited to see my son do extracurricular activities, but I'm not looking forward to the tween years. That just can't be pretty.

Let's face it, we don't want to embarrass our children, but we're really dressing for the other parents at these events—and, of course, for ourselves. A sporting event is a great place to bond with your child and his or her friends, and it's a good way to get to know the other parents. If you're single, it's a perfect place to meet single dads. Just make sure they are single. Really sure and really single. The dress code is relaxed, but you can still look spectacular.

Be casual. A school event is not the place to tart it up; there are children here, for goodness sake. And there's no need to alienate the other moms.

What You Should Wear

JEANS/CARGO PANTS: Be comfortable and chic. In the summer, Bermuda shorts and clam diggers are ideal options. Boyfriend jeans are a simple, no-fuss choice with sneakers and a sweater. Cargo pants look great with sneakers and a track jacket. No poom-poom shorts, ladies.

TOP: Wear a top that's weather appropriate and weekend-y. Maybe a polo or sailor style.

JACKET: A fitted leather jacket, a track jacket (very casual/hip), or a puffer coat if it's cold. The idea is sporty all-American, but never soccer mom.

SHOES: Sneakers or boots. Wellies with jeans or shorts are a spot-on spring look. Be practical; it's silly to wear heels, right?

BAG: For a sporting event, bring a tote to carry water and other sundries. At a play, a handbag is sufficient.

Don't bother with a ton of accessories or heavy makeup. Be toned down, natural, and comfortable. Be sporty, as it were.

WHAT'S in YOUR bag?

A snack or two and a bottle of water. Don't forget your sunglasses, some SPF, and a camera. Maybe some hand sanitizer. Not a bad idea to bring your business cards; you never know—someone's daddy might be Puff Daddy.

DON'TS FOR THE MOM AS SPECTATOR

- DON'T BE A MILF. Just be a regular mom.
- DON'T LAUGH IN THE WRONG PLACE during the play and don't insult the other children on the athletic field.
- DON'T BE A SORE LOSER. You're setting an example here.
- DON'T BE AFRAID TO CLAP THE LONGEST AND CHEER THE LOUDEST FOR YOUR BABY. And maybe give your kid a homemade trophy or Oscar at the end of the season (only in the privacy of your own home, of course). Be proud to be proud.

It's not whether you win or lose, it's how you play the game. Activities such as these teach our kids about some of life's most fundamental lessons, and they give you a chance to kick back from the hustle of your grown-up life and revel, if only for an afternoon, in the joy of being a kid. Isn't it exciting to see your baby on the field or on the stage doing his or her thing? They grow up so fast. You have to make the most of every single moment.

rule breakers we love

Venus and Serena Williams

Obviously, these girls make their parents proud. Both are phenomenal athletes and they have broken so many barriers in women's tennis—the game and the fashion. Venus and Serena are powerful role models for you and your children: strong, independent, and they love clothes. They're very nearly perfect.

Youth Gone Wild

What to Wear to Chaperone a School Dance

Adolescence is just one big walking pimple.

CAROL BURNETT

Thankfully, the prospect of my chaperoning a school dance is still in the very distant future. I can only imagine what a fascinating and terrifying event this is for a parent to witness: the hormones, the dramas, and enough eye-rolling to last you a lifetime. You need to show that you're cool yet in charge; you've *got* to have the right outfit to carry you through the night; and you certainly don't want to embarrass your teenager any more than necessary. It's bad enough you're the one who's chaperoning the dance.

What exactly should this ensemble say? It has to relay a subtly layered message: "I'm a cool mom but don't let me catch you breaking any rules, and I don't tolerate back talk." If you happen to be a single parent, you may want it to say, "I'm a cool, attractive, single mom." But be very careful to avoid treading into cougar territory; that's just inappropriate. Overall, dress modestly and relatively unobtrusively. Chaperones are supposed to remain in the background, unnoticed, and only step to the fore if a fight breaks out, if there's too much bumping and grinding on the dance floor, if you see someone smoking, or if you catch someone spiking the punch.

> *If you've never been hated by your child, you've never been a parent.*
>
> BETTE DAVIS

This is the ideal opportunity to observe your child in his or her natural habitat, while getting to know some of the other parents and teachers on a friendlier level. Think of the evening as a minicourse in social anthropology and have fun with it.

rule breakers we love

Katy Perry

Katy Perry has revived the pinup look and given it a modern twist. Everything she wears is fun and unexpected. I love a gorgeous, talented girl who can laugh at herself. A sense of humor is a style must.

You can definitely up your cool factor with the teens if you are well versed in what they're listening to. However, it's a fine line between cool and creepy—if you clearly are not someone who listens to hip-hop, don't front (as I just did by trying to use the lingo).

If you think you can handle the sights and sounds of chaperoning a high school party, wear comfortable shoes and get some earplugs. Dress according to the formality of the dance, but differentiate yourself from the teenage guests. A low-cut LBD is not appropriate for a school dance. You don't have to buy a prom dress to chaperone the prom, just be festive.

If the dance is casual, you can be too. Jeans are OK, but try to wear a pair that's a little sophisticated—not "Mom jeans," *never* "Mom jeans"—just avoid anything baggy, shredded, or teenage-y. Never wear anything that makes you look as though you could be one of the students. Leave the Ed Hardy and Rocawear at home.

Before you both head out, have your child give you a once-over and his or her stamp of approval; it's a wonderful bonding moment. Remember, many runway looks are born in the high schools of America, so you'll be able to gather fashion forward ideas while you're standing around for the next several hours.

Finally, even if your child is "freaking" on the dance floor, don't you freak out. Teenagers will be teenagers; as long as the lines of communication are open, everything will be OK.

WHAT'S in YOUR bag?

Bring a sewing kit (just a little one, in case some girl's strap breaks), a first aid kit, earplugs, and some Excedrin. OK, you're set.

Genius without education is like silver in the mine.

BENJAMIN FRANKLIN

Pomp and Circumstance

What to Wear to Your Child's Graduation

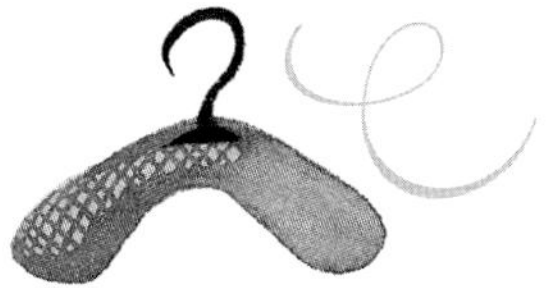

When I was a child, we had only two graduation ceremonies, high school and college. Now it seems like there's one every few years: pre-school, kindergarten, elementary school, middle school. . . . Of course, high school and college are still the two biggies. The thrill of watching the child you raised step into adulthood is moving and thought-provoking. The caps and gowns, the fresh, smiling faces: It'll make you want to call an old friend and get Botox all at once. So many milestones, so little time, and so many celebratory outfits to plan.

The earlier or "demi" graduations, as I like to call them, aren't seriously formal events. But it's always nice to give your graduate a morale boost by dressing up a bit. Buy him or her a graduation outfit, and you'll not only be known as the fashionista in their life, but you'll also both be picture perfect for the occasion.

High school graduation is a BIG deal. It is the culmination of twelve years of primary education and the doorway to adulthood. After the ceremony, there's usually a nice lunch or dinner, and in the best cases, a huge party. Dress up for this one; you've earned it. You should congratulate yourself as much as your child. You did it. You survived the teens. That's like completing the Iron Man. Reward yourself with a gorgeous, festive ensemble worthy of this celebration and show your child that the reason they have come this far is in large part because of their fabulous, gorgeous mom. Fete it up. Be colorful. Embrace patterns. Just don't be like the vampy aunt who shows up and hits on all the seniors.

College graduation is still a big deal, a really big deal, and festive attire is most definitely a must, but when this graduation rolls around, you may be feeling it in your bank account. A whole new outfit may not sound quite as doable as it did before four years of tuition payments. And there's a good chance you'll be traveling for this one. You might want to plan a versatile look, as there are often several components to this event: The actual graduation could be in the morning, you may have an afternoon reception to attend, and there's the celebratory dinner, followed by the parties. The crowd is young, fun, and ready to take on the world. If you're going to celebrate that with this crew, your outfit's got to work.

THE coif THE face

Go for a humidity-proof coif that's not too high; you don't want to obstruct anyone's view. Your makeup should be tear-proof. (You know you're going to cry.) Congratulations, Mom. Surviving your child's adolescence alone should merit a medal of valor. Give yourself a pat on the back and have a glass of bubbly in your own honor.

What You Should Wear

SEPARATES: Most graduations take place in May or June, so pretty summer separates or a dress is the rule. Bear in mind that you'll be sitting for quite a while, so avoid wrinkly fabrics or binding cuts. Graduation is a rite of passage for everyone in the family—you start planning for it from your child's birth. Wear something dignified to honor your child's accomplishment. Something like relaxed but elegant beige or taupe trousers in a lightweight fabric. A lovely white, or pastel-colored, scalloped shirt with just a bit of oomph, maybe a ruffled collar or interesting seaming. Swap the trousers for a tulip skirt.

JACKET: Bring a jacket or sweater. Even if it's hot outside, you never know when you'll encounter ferocious AC. Choose something a little unstructured that looks as good thrown over your arm as it does over your shoulders.

SHOES: Feminine sandals. When you're not sitting, you'll probably be walking, so make sure they're comfortable. And make sure you have a good pedicure.

ACCESSORIES: Wear sentimental jewelry. Set the whole look off with an unusual belt or textured hosiery.

BAG: Carry a good handbag that's roomy enough to fit everything you'll need for a full day. If you're traveling, use a pretty clutch as your cosmetics case and swap it out for dinner. As always, no logos.

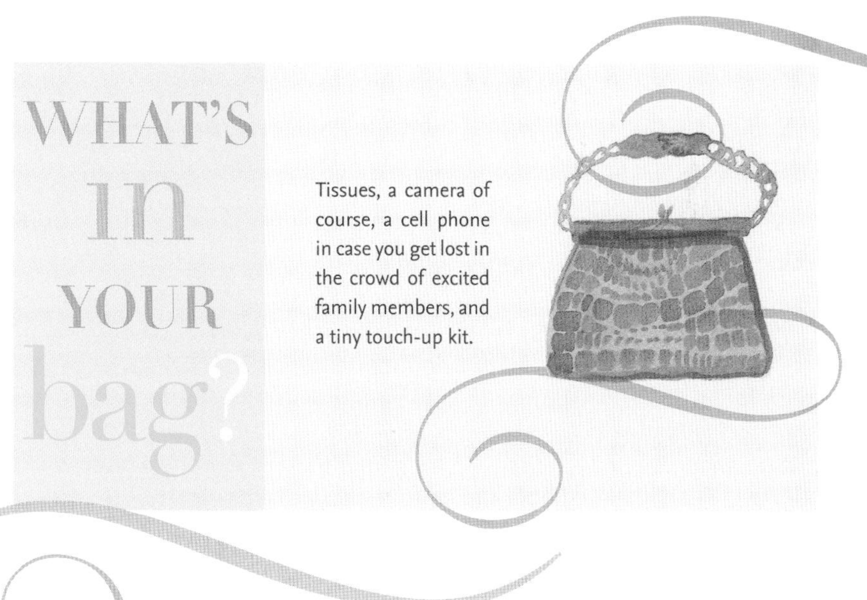

Tissues, a camera of course, a cell phone in case you get lost in the crowd of excited family members, and a tiny touch-up kit.

Objection, Your Honor

What to Wear to Jury Duty

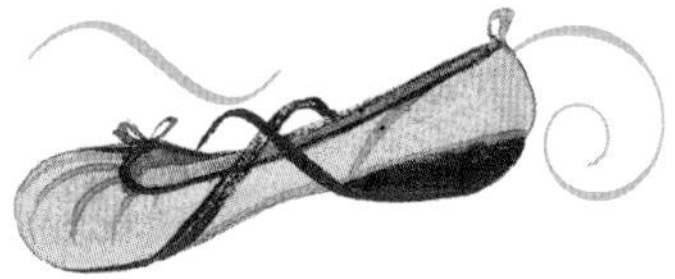

Almost all crime is due to the repressed desire for aesthetic expression.

EVELYN WAUGH

Ah, jury duty. Two words we all dread. But it's our civic responsibility, and one of the wonderful aspects of being an American is our right to a trial with a jury of our peers. And let's face it, jury duty is a fascinating little slice of life, with its motley crew of personalities, everyone as equally annoyed to be there as you are—almost like a Wednesday in high school. But somehow or another, you get into it, you people-watch, and if you're lucky, you learn a thing or two. Waiting to be called for consideration for seating on a jury and actually sitting (the operative word here is sitting) on the jury involve spending a great deal of time in uncomfortable seats. Be prepared.

Another important consideration: You never know who you might meet in the jury pool—an old friend, a cute boy, an ex-boyfriend, his new girl, a potential employer, or a potential client. Dress as you would for a casual workday. This is a perfect opportunity to break in those uncomfortable heels, since you won't be doing much walking.

BEST-DRESSED COURTROOM DRAMAS

These films offer an array of beautifully dressed women. Take notes.

- *Witness for the Prosecution:* Just for Marlene Dietrich's gorgeous costumes.
- *Anatomy of a Murder:* In this classic film, saucy Lee Remick gets a prim makeover for her trial.
- *Written on the Wind:* Upstanding Lauren Bacall and blousy Dorothy Malone both look fantastic in the trial scene—a great reference.
- *Adam's Rib:* Katharine Hepburn looks amazing in every film she's in; this one is no exception.
- *Primal Fear:* A gripping drama featuring a courtroom scene with a crisply turned-out Laura Linney and a more down-to-earth Frances McDormand, and stellar performances by the entire cast.

If you are eager to become an active participant in the legal process, it is best to keep your look simple and conservative. You don't want to appear at all extreme—not too rich, too artsy, or too eccentric. And quite frankly, you don't want the defendant to pay particular attention to you. I knew a woman who was being considered as a juror in a drug-related murder trial, many years ago, and the defendants (I don't pre-judge but this is an example of what NOT to wear if you are being tried for a drug-related murder) looked like they walked off the set of *Law & Order*, as the bad guys—and they were taking a lot of notes throughout the jury selection. The moral of the story here is that everyone is looking at everyone else in a courtroom—usually because sitting around is incredibly boring—so make it your business to look moderately smart and sensibly pretty.

However, if you really want to avoid jury duty this time around, you increase your chances of being excused by dressing more suggestively, very eccentrically, or as if your outfit were laid out by your butler that morning. Think in extremes, such as leopard or some other animal print, or bright color and a loud graphic print. Make them wonder who the hell you are. Wear bold makeup—colorful eye shadows or bright lips—that says you're not really the kind of girl who wants to think about weighty judicial matters.

> *Only lawyers and mental defectives are automatically exempt from jury duty.*
>
> GEORGE BERNARD SHAW

WHAT'S in YOUR bag?

Fit whatever you can into this bag; it's going to be a long day. Crossword puzzles, snacks, water, books, knitting, a *fully charged* iPhone or BlackBerry, maybe a journal. You're in for the long haul.

Good Mourning

What to Wear to a Funeral

After great pain a formal feeling comes

EMILY DICKINSON

I almost hate the idea of writing about death and fashion in the same paragraph, but people have to dress for funerals, and I want to point out that this moment of solemn acknowledgment really should be dignified by a nod to decorum from all of the guests—including you. Funerals are a time for reflection, a moment to look at mortality face-to-face, to honor those who have passed on, and to comfort the bereaved. After a funeral, we come home feeling more grateful for the wonderful things in our lives.

A JAZZ FUNERAL

At a New Orleans funeral, family, friends, and a jazz band all move from the funeral home to the cemetery while the band plays a dirge. After the burial, the band launches into upbeat music while the procession marches to another location to dance and celebrate the life of the deceased.

Black is no longer mandatory for funerals, but I don't recommend wearing a party dress. Funerals are for those closest to the dearly departed; your number one consideration should be to respect them and dress in a way that you know they will appreciate.

As a rule, think plain, unadorned, gravitas. No cleavage, thigh-high boots, or microminis. No animal prints and certainly no cowboy fringe. Your best bet is to stick with neutrals or darker colors. Definitely avoid bright floral prints or loud colors like neon pink. As long as your palette is relatively subdued you should be fine. And when in doubt—just wear black.

> *Funeral pomp is more for the vanity of the living than for the honor of the dead.*
>
> FRANÇOIS DE LA ROCHEFOUCAULD

THE coif THE face

Hair should be neat and away from the face. You want to be able to look people in the eyes. Try a polished ponytail or a loose, side-swept bun. Makeup should be the bare minimum. Use tear-proof mascara and lip stain that won't smudge your Kleenex as you blot the inevitable tear.

rule breakers we love

Queen Alexandra

Consort of Edward VII, Alexandra of Denmark is credited with popularizing clothing in colors like sugar almond and sweet pea (which sound intriguingly delicious). She scandalized England by wearing a light-colored dress to her 1901 coronation when most were still wearing black in mourning for the late Queen Victoria. A trendsetter, not a trend follower.

LIFE AFTER DEATH

- IN NORTHERN VIETNAM, families disinter the bones of deceased relatives and rebury them in the family garden or in other family land.
- IN HALLSTATT, AUSTRIA, after twelve years, the family disinters the remains of their deceased relatives and decorates their skulls, which are then displayed in a chapel.
- IN GHANA, it's popular to be buried in a "fantasy coffin," which is decorated to represent how the deceased lived his or her life. It could be a car or an airplane or any other object.
- IN SWEDEN, an organization called Promessa Organic AB is planning a prometrium where the deceased will go through an eco-friendly process of freeze-drying; when the body has been reduced to a fine powder, the metals that were in the body are extracted and recycled, and the remains are buried in a biodegradable coffin.

This is a tough time. Be a rock for your loved ones. Exchange a lot of hugs and condolences. Cry if you need to.

weddings

Spoken For

What to Wear to Your Engagement Party

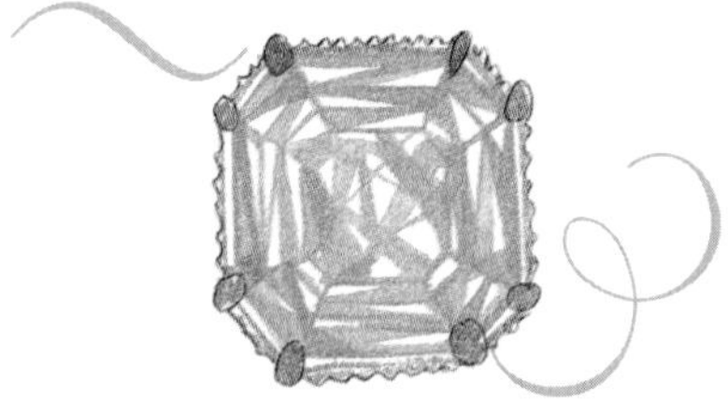

I never worry about diets. The only carrots that interest me are the number you get in a diamond.

MAE WEST

Traditionally, an engagement party is thrown by the bride's parents, and in addition to announcing the exciting news to your nearest and dearest, it's an opportunity for the two families to meet and begin building a beautiful and lasting relationship. A lifelong merger, if you will.

Since everyone invited to the engagement party is expected to be invited to the wedding, this affair kicks off the mood of the Big Day. If you're a traditional girl, by all means, hand over the guest list, let your parents do their duty, and just show up glowing. Festive is the word and bubbly is the mood. The butterflies in your stomach will have you virtually walking on air for this soiree. You'll be high on life, and your style will accentuate your radiance.

Many of my friends have opted for two separate parties: a traditional engagement party for their parents and extended families and another, less formal affair, for friends and coworkers. Unlike in politics, this two-party system is a great, low-stress way to accommodate the old school and the new school. There is absolutely no reason you can't wear the same dress to both parties—only your fiancé will know. It's so easy to create two completely different looks by mixing up the trimmings, such as shoes and accessories. However, if you can't resist the lure of having a great excuse to get another dress, go for it. Be a total princess if you like. Create an entire trousseau just for the wedding-related events.

> *Glamour is what makes a man ask for your phone number. But it is also what makes a woman ask for the name of your dressmaker.*
>
> LILLY DACHÉ

Rule number one: Wear a party dress (or dresses) that you love. In fact, wear a party dress that radiates love. This landmark moment in your life's trajectory calls for a transcendent look, a statement. Not only do you get to wear a showstopping ensemble, you are expected to. The bliss of your newfound love and commitment will emanate from you as some sort of magical, shimmering fairy dust

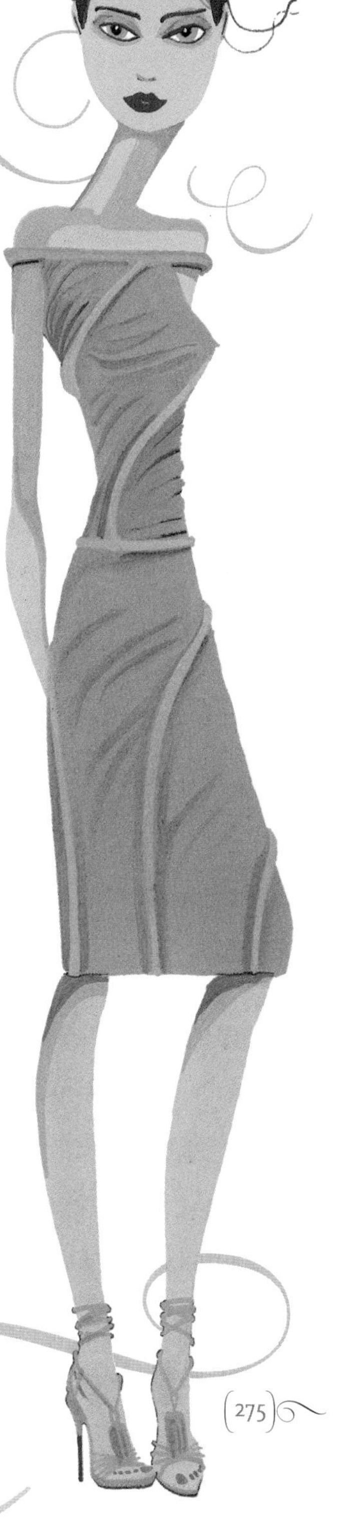

reserved only for fiancés and brides. In the right dress, you might even float. Put together a polished, celebratory look that represents the best of your taste and style.

Your engagement party regalia is a personal choice, and there are many variables: day, night, traditional, casual, spring, summer, winter, fall, and on and on. I'm going to provide some basic inspiration and leave the details up to you. Remember: This moment is yours. It is 100 percent, completely, and unabashedly YOURS. Own it and indulge in it.

> *Love is a game that two can play and both win.*
>
> EVA GABOR

What You Should Wear

SEPARATES: Flowy, wide-leg trousers in a silky fabric are a fantastic, versatile option to a dress or skirt. A sleek halter with sequins or beading, or a strapless corset-style top sets off soft, relaxed trousers perfectly. Or consider a pair of super skinny pants in a luxurious brocade, with a ruffled, high-collared satin blouse and a cropped, fitted jacket reminiscent of Alexander McQueen. Play with textures and silhouette; it's a great way to bring added interest to your ensemble. Mix matte and shiny, hard and soft, tailored and relaxed. If you balance these elements, you will avoid looking sloppy or stiff, too shiny or too dull—and you'll stand out from the crowd.

DRESS: Elegant, frothy, billowy, with just a smidge of sexy siren; it's a good idea to choose something that can do double duty for day or evening. This should be a breeze if you're resourceful with your accessories. Since you're soon going to be a bride, with all the pomp and grandeur that entails, luxuriate now in a chance to be the natural, beautiful woman that you are. You want a flirty dress that accentuates your assets without holding you back from dancing, eating, and, of course, showing off the ring.

SHOES: Splurge on your shoes. Buy a pair that will be your go-to party shoes for the year—fun, fancy, and a little decadent.
ACCESSORIES: It's all in the accessories, ladies. The engagement ring is your statement piece for the evening; that's the real focus. Cuff links accent a beautiful ring perfectly. They're just a touch of glitz at the wrist without competing with the main attraction.
BAG: An adorable clutch. If you're wearing black, a sparkly, colorful bag is a perfect accent. If you're wearing a strong color, choose a neutral or black bag with a bit of beading.

A DIAMOND IN THE ROUGH

Every girl should know her diamonds. We've all heard of the four Cs: cut, color, clarity, carats. Here's a quick primer on those characteristics. And remember, natural fancy-colored diamonds are rare, so don't expect one unless your fiancé's last name is Onassis.

- CUT: Round, Oval, Sapphire, Princess, Marquise, Radiant, Cushion, Emerald, Pear, Asscher
- COLOR: Anywhere from clear (highest quality) to canary (still good)
- FANCY COLOR: Champagne, green, pink, and blue
- CLARITY: This refers to any flaws, such as inclusions or irregularities in the diamond. Usually these flaws are invisible to the naked eye and only affect the value of the diamond rather than its appearance.
- CARAT: A unit of weight for gemstones equal to 200 mg.

---

rule breakers we love

Anita Loos

She penned the famous line "Diamonds are a girl's best friend" in her book, later turned lavish musical, *Gentlemen Prefer Blondes,* starring Jane Russell and Marilyn Monroe. Ms. Loos authored many of the movies and plays that have come to embody the witty, Technicolor best of the fifties.

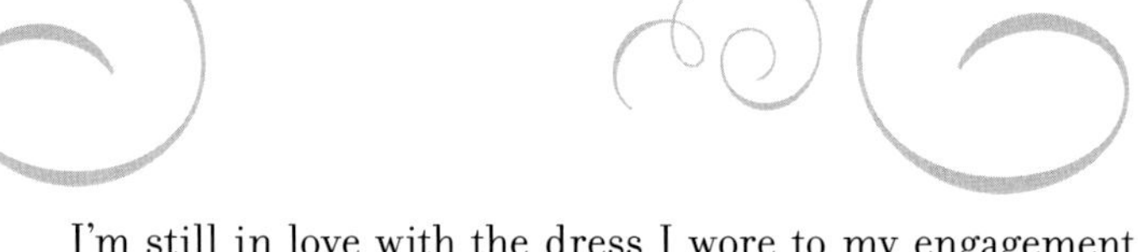

I'm still in love with the dress I wore to my engagement party, and I have since worn it many times. For your soiree, raw silk is a wonderful option, a gorgeous, semi-luxe fabric that works for any season. It has a hint of sheen and a touch of texture, and comes in breathtaking colors. An added benefit, raw silk has enough body to conceal what you want concealed while still draping beautifully. In fact, I might just go out and get a few yards now and have a little conversation with my tailor—I'm inspired. I'm envisioning a strapless number, with a fitted bodice, and a perfectly hip-skimming pencil skirt ending just below the knee. With a simple cut, you can go for a striking, vivacious color like deep turquoise or very dark violet. Accessorize with a simple necklace and earrings and keep your wrists bare—remember, emphasize that ring finger.

For a more playful look, you can try a short-sleeved dress in a wide nautical stripe, with a boat neck, a fitted bodice, nipped in at the waist, and a full skirt with pockets. Fresh and pretty. At the risk of sounding like a broken record, I'll remind you of January Jones in *Mad Men*; any one of her evening looks is perfect for a chic engagement party.

ENGAGEMENT PARTY *DO'S*

- GO FOR PRETTY OVER VAMPY. Today you are a blossom, an angel; a short (but not too short) skirt or hint of décolletage is fine, but save vampy for the bachelorette party.
- EMBRACE FLORALS. A bouquet of color adds life and vibrancy.
- A BASIC, NEUTRAL MANICURE IS A MUST. You want to show off that rock with no distractions. Keep your hands baby soft by covering them with heavy moisturizer and putting on cotton gloves before bed; this works for feet too, with socks instead of gloves.
- CHAMPAGNE IS ALSO A MUST.

Let's not kid ourselves: Wedding planning can be a nightmare. You may find, after numerous conversations with your mom, you're questioning your own sanity. And you'll definitely discover that losing ten pounds before the wedding is not going to be so easy. You freak out, you panic (and in my case eat even more); don't despair, everything is going to be perfection.

Every woman has dreamy expectations about how her wedding will play out, and you can lose your mind trying to keep everyone else happy. So while you have this sacred time of newness and possibilities, ENJOY IT. Bask in the pre-planning congratulations and do nothing but have a fabulous time. Bring everyone you love together and don't worry about whether or not they're getting along. This night is about you and your fiancé; you're embarking on an exciting future together. Live it up. And congratulations!

Last Whirl with the Girls

What to Wear to Your Bachelorette Party

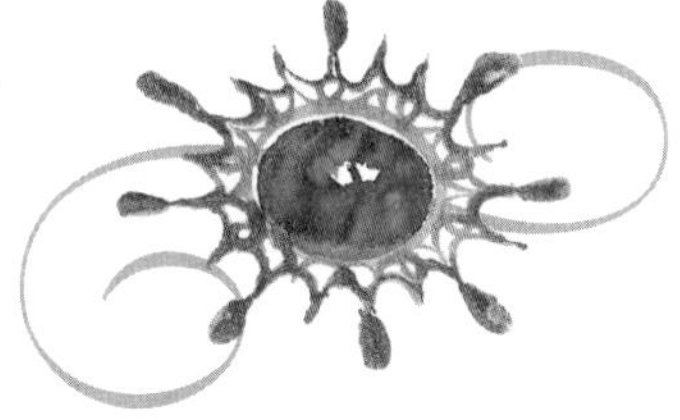

Exuberance is better than taste.

GUSTAVE FLAUBERT

The infamous bachelorette party. Your last hurrah as a single girl. The feeling on this occasion is jubilation with your girlfriends, dolled up and ready to party. There are no rules on this night (the stories to come from this outing may become the stuff of legend!). Set aside the stress of wedding planning, the frustrating interpersonal struggles that have arisen between family and friends, and the general tying of loose ends as the big day approaches. Get crazy and have a blast.

rule breakers we love

Elizabeth Taylor

Elizabeth Taylor is in love with love. She's famous for her drama, her marriages, and her stunning violet eyes. She also loves diamonds and bijoux and has been lucky enough to receive her fair share of gorgeous jewels. Liz's portrayal of Cleopatra is iconic because the two have so much in common. They are strong, independent, beautiful women who know what they want, know how to get it, and know how to wear jewelry.

Sometimes I bust out and do things so permanent. Like tattoos and marriage.

DREW BARRYMORE

THE *DO'S*

- MAKE IT CLEAR TO YOUR MAID OF HONOR WHAT YOU ARE, AND ARE NOT, COMFORTABLE WITH. These affairs sometimes focus on embarrassing the bride to be. It's vital that this party is fun for *you*.
- CONSIDER A COED BACHELOR/BACHELORETTE PARTY. An excellent way to avoid pre-wedding lovers' quarrels.
- COME UP WITH AN ACTIVITY OR THEME FOR THE EVENING, like salsa dancing, casino night, or my personal favorite, wine tasting.
- HAVE A HANGOVER REMEDY AVAILABLE FOR EVERYONE AT THE END OF THE NIGHT. I'm told that Boozer really works; it can't hurt, right?

It's your night to be a diva, your night to look like you are capable of making a grown man cry. Wear what makes you feel like the hottest girl in the room. Whatever you thought was too much for the engagement party is perfect. Tonight, outrageous is fine.

What You Should Wear

SEPARATES: See above. Be playful, you're with your girlfriends. Anything goes! Shorts with tights and outrageous stilettos, cigarette pants, tuxedos. . . . Wear them with a sequined tank or a daring, plunging V-neck.
DRESS: As short or as low cut as you dare. Don something slinky and fun. Be festive, be whimsical, be edgy, whatever you fancy. A colorful, sparkly number à la Gucci, Balmain, or Emilio Pucci is tantalizing. It's your last chance to party like a teenager—at least, for a while.
SHOES: Get out your dancing shoes. Even if you aren't planning on going dancing, you never know where the evening will lead. High heels, boots, booties, strappy sandals, choose whatever makes you look and feel like a star.

HOSIERY: Sometimes strappy heels and microminis are just too much, even for a bachelorette party. Slip on a pair of opaque tights and you're golden. Or try a pair of fishnets with a longer skirt (fishnets and a micromini tend toward vulgar).

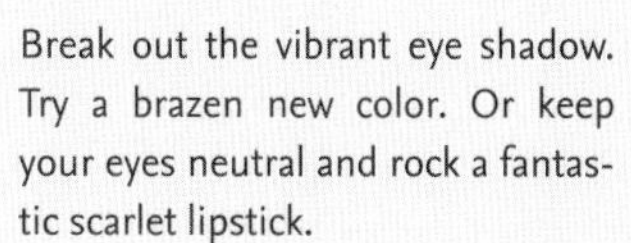

I'm getting giddy just thinking about all of the spectacular options for your bachelorette party gear. Wear your glitziest costume jewelry, an oversize cocktail ring, a chunky bracelet. I had a friend who received a huge faux diamond ring that doubled as a shot glass at her bachelorette party. I've never seen women more enamored with a piece of paste jewelry in my life. Taste is irrelevant tonight. Dress for an evening of clubbing and channel your inner Rihanna. Be fierce.

Since I can't come over and help you get dressed, call a friend. Have a few pre-party cocktails and do each other's makeup—just like the old days. Now go out and have the time of your life (don't do anything I wouldn't do). And remember, "What happens in Vegas stays in Vegas" may be a thing of the past! These days "What happens in Vegas winds up on Facebook." Have fun, but . . . do keep that in mind.

Ladies Who Lunch

What to Wear to a Bridal Shower

As Daddy said, life is ninety-five percent anticipation.

GLORIA SWANSON

Bridal Shower. These two words evoke tradition and femininity, a time for girls to get together and be girls. What's better than spending an afternoon with your closest friends over an elegant brunch celebrating your impending marriage? You really have everything you need: wonderful friends, delicious food, juicy wedding gossip, and great style. And, of course, gifts.

Whenever a woman asks me what she should wear to a bridal shower, I envision Grace Kelly in a garden wearing a full-skirted frock with loads of crinolines and a constructed bodice, surrounded by mountains of beautifully wrapped gifts.

Then I come back to reality.

A bridal shower is often an afternoon or early evening event. It definitely calls for a pretty dress. So let's make the mood "afternoon garden party" and work from there. It's a plus if you can start with a motif as a touchstone for style inspiration. You are the belle of this ball. Wear something colorful and beautiful, and embody the excitement of your upcoming wedding.

THE SHOWER STORY

- The bridal shower is a relatively new tradition; it gained popularity as recently as the late seventeenth or early eighteenth century (seventeenth century is recent in a historical context).
- In the Victorian era, women filled Japanese parasols with gifts that showered down upon the bride-to-be when she opened them. A lovely idea; the Victorians came up with so many pretty traditions. We should revive this one.
- In the twenties, bridal showers were supposed to be a complete surprise. A couple of the bride-to-be's friends would distract her with an outing, while other friends filled her house with gifts as a surprise when she returned. Also a darling custom.

What You Should Wear

SEPARATES: If you're not a spring dress kind of girl, go for separates. In keeping with the Grace Kelly motif, cashmere twinsets in ice-creamy colors keep popping into my head. That's taking traditional entirely too far. However, wide-leg trousers—either slouchy linen or silk, or sharply creased light wool—are comfortably sophisticated. Try a silky blouse with a feminine touch, such as exaggerated, poufy sleeves; or a crisp cotton, sleeveless shell with an origami detail; perhaps an invigorating print. Take a cue from Nicole Kidman's classic yet fashion forward style, or Anne Hathaway's youthful and modern approach to dressing.

DRESS: *Do* think Grace Kelly! Why not? I still envision a fitted bodice with a full skirt. No crinolines though, just some gathers, perhaps a few pleats or pin tucks, and a ruffle or two. A bridal shower look should be ladylike and easy to move in. Bright spring colors or festive florals are always welcome. You're a blossom and life is a bed of roses, so dress for it.

COAT: A swing coat or a light trench. They work in just about any weather and look divine with everything.

SHOES: If ever any look screamed for a delicious pair of ballet flats, this is it. Repetto, of course. And a pretty pair of Mary Janes is a perfectly acceptable alternative. Prada, Chloé, or any look that's a modern take on vintage-inspired style. Espadrilles are a wonderful spring option; they're easy chic.

ACCESSORIES: Accentuate your waist with a pretty belt, and showcase your swanlike neck with a simple necklace. Or wear a charm bracelet for luck. Ultimately, though, that fabulous engagement ring is still your best accessory.

BAG: A modest handbag fits the bill perfectly.

Whatever you wear, your ecstatic glow is your second-best bridal shower accessory (after the ring). Enjoy the girl talk and relax with your friends for a few hours. Forget about fitting into your wedding dress; revel in your princess status (it doesn't last forever). Treasure every step of your journey. These memories will last a lifetime.

ECO-FRIENDLY PARTY FAVORS

- Seating or thank-you cards with seeds inside to plant
- Flower bulbs in decorative (recycled) tissue with ribbon
- Mini bamboo plants
- Sachets

Love Is in the Wear

What to Wear to a Rehearsal Dinner

Context and memory play powerful roles in all the truly great meals in one's life.

ANTHONY BOURDAIN

Can you believe it? You've miraculously survived almost all the planning and coordinating; the out-of-town guests from Thailand to Texas have all started to arrive; and you've just rehearsed your WEDDING. Take a few deep breaths and let the butterflies in your stomach have a savasana. It's all starting to feel more real now. You are actually getting married. This is your last dress-up affair before the ultimate in dress-up affairs. And, ever the style maven, you want to look perfect.

One of the most entertaining rehearsal dinners I've heard of was an outdoor seafood buffet on Cape Cod. Fresh seafood alone makes an amazing dinner party. The bride was Italian American and the groom was Irish; as a nod to the two cultures, they had wine (plenty of it!) and a Celtic band. There may even have been a piñata, which has nothing to do with Italy or Ireland, but a piñata is always fun. The bride wanted to enjoy the party from the moment they arrived, so they didn't all sit down together for a formal dinner; instead, the party was an ongoing extravaganza. Thank goodness she had the foresight to plan an evening wedding; the rehearsal dinner was a late night.

What You Should Wear

DRESS: The goal is to bring a tear to everyone's eye and make the groom's heart skip a beat as you enter the room. First consider how formal the dinner will be, then decide what look you are going for. You can't go wrong with elegant sophistication. This dress should reflect the momentousness of the occasion and it should make you feel wonderful. If the thought of creating yet another flawless ensemble is overwhelming amid all of the last-minute details, why not rework your engagement party outfit with different accessories? So easy, and you already know it looks great.

COAT: Obviously the weather plays a part in your decision, but go for something unexpected—perhaps a feminized tuxedo jacket, or a sleek blazer.

SHOES: Don't wear uncomfortable shoes; rest your feet for tomorrow, when you'll be dancing for hours. That's not to say you should wear Birkenstocks, just nothing too high.

Don't get bent out of shape if some little detail goes awry at the rehearsal dinner. It's not that big a deal. Tonight you should eat, relax, and have a good cry with the ones you love. Take tons of pictures for your photo album and show poise and grace as you listen to those hilarious and heartwarming toasts. Take a moment to sit back in your chair and soak it all in. This is one of *those* moments, so cherish it. Now, stop crying and go get dressed, darling.

THE coif THE face

To complete your low-key glamour-girl look, keep your hair smooth and adorn it with a glittery clip. Your rosy glow of excitement may actually eliminate the need for cosmetics. But have a little fun; go for a daring eye shadow or bold liquid liner. Drama tonight (style drama not melodrama, of course). And remember to enjoy your rehearsal dinner while you can; for most of the rest of life's big occasions, you don't get to practice.

Age does not protect you from love,
but love, to some extent, protects you from age.

JEANNE MOREAU

rules are made to be broken

Never wear stockings with open-toed shoes.

Done right, open-toed shoes look fabulous with stockings. The key is wearing pretty, high quality hosiery in any color other than nude. A glimpse of well-pedicured toes under a lace or fishnet stocking is edgy and alluring. Match your leg wear to your shoes for a sophisticated look; if you're feeling a bit daring, wear bright hosiery. And always walk on the cutting edge.

To Honor and Adorn

What to Wear to a Black-Tie Wedding

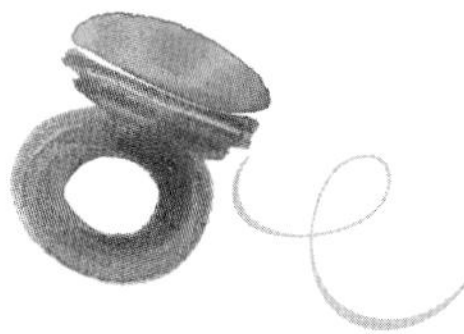

Dressing up. People just don't do it anymore. We need to change that.

JOHN GALLIANO

A black-tie wedding is the ultimate formal occasion; it's simply impossible to be overdressed for this event. I personally adore a black-tie wedding. All those gems sparkling in the candlelight, caviar on ice, champagne. What's better than that?

Black tie can be a bit daunting for the uninitiated (even for the seasoned partygoers among us), and sometimes it's just annoying to dress black tie. But rethink this hassle as a fun style exercise. Make it your personal challenge to come up with a quintessential black-tie look, a gorgeous ensemble that gets you safely through a long and complex evening in one piece. You will do a lot of standing; you will do a lot of sitting; and you will be shaking a lot of hands and exchanging abundant air kisses and careful, "don't mush my gown" hugs. You will also be doing a lot of dancing, drinking, and eating. Socializing is a must; comfort is a luxury, but an attainable luxury.

So exciting! Everyone's looking their absolute best and you're celebrating the loving union of two wonderful people whom you love, or at least have met once or twice. This is a style marathon, ladies; you've got to train for it, and you must have the proper equipment. You must be able to stand in your heels without wincing, sit in your dress without worrying about the strength of its seams, and, most important, you must turn heads.

BLACK-TIE WEDDING *DON'TS*

- DON'T WEAR WHITE. Never upstage the bride. Even if you know she won't be wearing it, white is too fraught with symbolism on this day.
- DON'T WEAR DARK LIPSTICK. Opt for scarlet lips at your own risk and be prepared for frequent mirror checks if you do. (Besides, there is nothing sexier than a dark eye and a pale lip.)
- DON'T WEAR ANYTHING SKINTIGHT OR TOO REVEALING. The look is elegant and glamorous, not stripper chic.

The key to pulling off a black-tie look is not a $5,000 dress (although it helps) or following strict rules of etiquette. Most of us don't have an unlimited budget or an endless array of gowns to choose from, so deciding what to wear is surprisingly simple. The hard part is owning your look and maintaining an air of, "This old thing? I throw this on to go grocery shopping," while conveying all of the joy and formality of the occasion.

Formal in the Afternoon and Formal at Night

A beautiful black-tie look for an afternoon wedding is a flirty, floral print dress in a sumptuous fabric with a fitted bodice and a full, cocktail-length skirt for twirling on the dance floor. Or, if you want to keep things simple, wear a dashing LBD with a bit of jet-beading or lace embellishment. Perhaps a lavish brocade with fur trim or sumptuous velvet with gold accents. For drama, look to Louis Vuitton, Oscar de la Renta, or Christian Lacroix; for sophistication, YSL or Dior; and for romance, Miu Miu and Chloé are inspirational.

An evening wedding is the consummate occasion for a breathtaking gown. How often do you have an excuse to showcase a gown? Not a stiff, corseted, red-carpet dress, of course, but a stunning and classically draped creation. Vionnet and Lanvin are goddess gown artists.

You are not required to wear stockings with formal wear. If the weather allows, a faux tan and a luxurious pedicure are all you need. If you want the coverage, choose an ultra-sheer, low-denier stocking.

THE coif THE face

When I'm going all-out formal, I wear my hair upswept in a chic chignon, or pulled back into a smooth ponytail. A low ponytail, mind you; we're not trying out for the cheerleading squad.

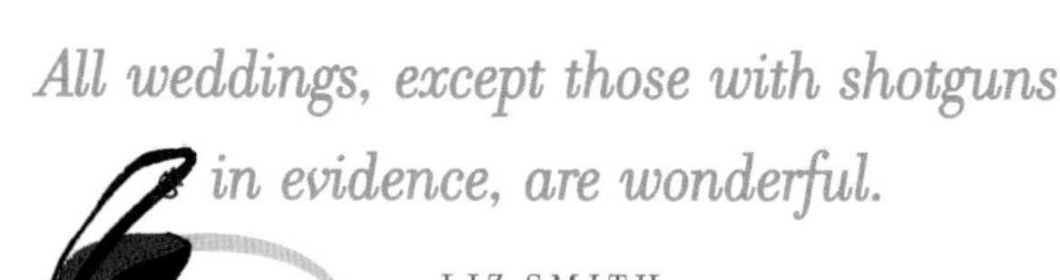

All weddings, except those with shotguns in evidence, are wonderful.

LIZ SMITH

The Shoe Biz

Strappy stilettos or metallic platforms are the perfect complement to a formal gown. A flash of color with every step achieves that sexy and elusive wow factor. I always wear new shoes around the house for a few days prior to taking them out on the town, and I strongly recommend you do the same. This is key for avoiding blisters and general shoe misery.

Day or evening, formal attire cannot work its magic without foundation garments. It's tempting to wear your sexiest lingerie under your fabulous evening dress, but practicality must take precedence. You don't want anything showing through that isn't intended to; nude or black is probably required. Spanx are a revelation; embrace them, own them, love them. Spanx never let me down. Or any *part* of me, for that matter.

Accessories

When the earrings are lavish, I leave my neck bare and throw on a cuff or a cocktail ring. When the earrings are small and simple, I drape myself in a statement necklace or two. You, my dear, should wear whatever makes you feel as unabashedly glamorous as you can possibly imagine.

SETTING THE MOOD: PURE ELEGANCE

- LISTEN TO THE SOUNDTRACK OF *BREAKFAST AT TIFFANY'S*: Henry Mancini is sublime. Follow it up with some Roy Orbison or Edith Piaf to set your heart racing.
- WATCH ANY MOVIE WITH AUDREY HEPBURN, the unrivaled queen of approachable elegance.
- FILL YOUR ROOM WITH FRESH-CUT FLOWERS. The colors and aromas will envelop you in the aura of new beginnings.
- RELAX WITH A CUP OF TEA OR A DRY MARTINI. Either beverage will center you (well, maybe not the martini) and imbue you with the appropriate vibe for black tie.

Once you've properly set the mood, and you're fully prepared with back-up shoes and an emergency sewing kit, you need to forget about what you look like and prepare to have fun.

Romance is the glamour that turns the dust of everyday life into a golden haze.

AMANDA CROSS

How to Be the Perfect Wedding Guest

- Have a light snack before you leave the house so you're not tempted to start eating fistfuls of appetizers.
- When you run out of things to say, throw out a compliment.
- Don't bring up politics, religion, or who you know previously dated the groom. Especially if you dated him.
- If your heels start to feel like they're getting higher or sprouting roller skates—switch from champagne to water.
- Don't dirty dance with the best man.

WEDDINGS THAT ENTRANCED US

- QUEEN VICTORIA, trendsetter that she was, popularized the white wedding dress and married Albert of Saxe-Coburg in 1840, wearing a white gown.
- PRINCE CHARLES AND LADY DI: A tragic ending, but probably the most watched wedding in history.
- TOM CRUISE AND KATIE HOLMES: Strange, but gorgeous and fascinating.
- GWEN STEFANI AND GAVIN ROSSDALE: Gwen was perfection in John Galliano. (She loved the dress so much, she wore it twice.)
- JOHN F. KENNEDY, JR., AND CAROLYN BESSETTE: Another tragic ending, but a beautiful wedding and a stunningly beautiful couple.
- GRACE KELLY AND PRINCE RAINIER III OF MONACO: Pure fairy-tale magic.

A Fine Romance

What to Wear to a Casual Wedding

Deserve your dream.

OCTAVIO PAZ

The angst of dressing for a wedding seems to lessen just a bit when we know we don't necessarily have to dress way up. The stakes go down; you can relax a little. Which is why I am such a fan of the casual wedding; it puts everyone—guests and couple alike—at ease. With everyone more laid back, the focus can be on the significance of the day, and on having a great time.

Casual weddings run the gamut from barefoot on the beach to slightly dressed up in a church. The invitation will give you the particulars about location, theme, and dress code. You just have to pull together your perfect look.

I'm often asked about what's appropriate for a theme wedding, be it beach, ethnic, or vintage. As a rule, a theme is just that, an overall tone. The happy couple doesn't want you to show up in a costume; they want their guests to reflect the flavor of their chosen motif, so that the affair will have a special character. The wedding party may have to go all out, but guests won't be expected to show up looking like they belong in Versailles.

What You Should Wear

Make your casual wedding ensemble chic but playful, and always err on the side of elegance. Casual or not, it is a wedding.

DRESS: Be flirty in a pink dress and matching lipstick, or any dress that's flirty and modern. Go a little sparkly with sequins or beading or keep it matte and relaxed with natural fabrics. Proenza Schouler and Marc Jacobs make to-die-for feminine dresses with a rock-and-roll vibe.

TROUSERS: Slouchy and silky trousers with an edgy vest; or tuxedo pants with a cropped bolero. Fluttery little shorts with a gauzy blouse or a long blazer are the perfect blend of girlie and casual, modern dressing. Think Chanel, Stella McCartney, Diane Kruger, and Kate Moss for laid-back, sophisticated style.

> *A successful marriage requires falling in love many times, always with the same person.*
>
> MIGNON MCLAUGHLIN

Use the invitation as a guide, find out how dressy your friends plan to be, and you're ready to strategize. It's always more fun, and easier, to shop with a girlfriend who's going to the same event. This way you can compare notes and boost each other's confidence.

Weddings sometimes come all in one season, don't they? If you've been invited to five casual weddings in one summer, you don't want to buy a completely new outfit for each wedding; what you want is a season's worth of dresses for the price of one. Find a basic sheath and change it up each time with new accessories or a different hairstyle. Black is OK for weddings, as long as you make it festive. However, color is much more exciting. Wear your dresses with different shoes, hosiery, jewelry, and jacket for each event.

JUMPING THE BROOM

Jumping the broom originated in West Africa. In Ashanti culture, brooms symbolize sweeping away evil spirits and are present in wedding ceremonies. In the United States, because slaves were forbidden to marry, the ritual of exchanging vows in front of a witness and then jumping over a broom together became a recognized marriage.

THE CANDLE CEREMONY

In Colombia, after the ring ceremony, the bride and groom each light a candle. They bring the two flames together to light a third candle and extinguish theirs. The single flame represents their union. To that I say, Come on, baby, light my fire.

If you're single, a casual wedding is the perfect place to get some digits while you mingle with the other unattached guests. If you're married, make it a nostalgic date night, then go home and relive your honeymoon. And if you bring a date, don't give him meaningful looks while the vows are being exchanged. That's a quick way to send him running in the other direction.

rule breakers we love

Pink

Pink's aggressive style is all over the map. Pasties, wifebeaters, shredded jeans, trapeze. She wore a voluminous white and black Monique Lhuillier gown with a crown of ringlets for her beach wedding. Completely unexpected. You want to say "What the...?" but instead you say "Wow."

Matriarchal Chic

What to Wear to Your Daughter's Wedding

If I know what love is,
it's because of you.

HERMANN HESSE

Your baby is getting married! You have a million things to do. Phone calls to make, parties to throw, menus to plan, guest lists to review, flowers to coordinate, and arguments with your daughter to win. And what are you going to wear? This is important—as important as the orchid arrangements you're losing sleep over. Remember that the wedding photos are going to wind up in albums for generations to come. You need an outfit worthy of ushering your beloved child into the next phase of her life.

Maybe you've been planning this outfit since the day you found out you were pregnant. If so, your look has probably gone through several revisions over the years. You may have wanted a floor-length Halston halter dress in the seventies, then a turquoise taffeta, off-the-shoulder creation with a bubble skirt in the eighties. A few years later, you may have seen yourself in a simple, bias-cut, empire-waist, aubergine column. Oh, how one's fashion perspective can change as trends come and go. Nonetheless, here you are, about to become a full-fledged mother-in-law. This is a night to wear what I like to call "an important dress."

rule breakers we love

Mrs. Robinson

Mrs. Robinson wasn't the nicest woman, but she had great style. Her chic gray streak and animal print lingerie accentuated her older and more experienced woman appeal, proving that there doesn't have to be anything matronly about being a mother-in-law.

The Important Dress

This is the kind of dress that a) looks very luxe, b) fits as if it were made just for you, and c) looks like royalty could have worn it. Even if the wedding is casual, you—the mother of the bride—are allowed to go all out if you want to. The happy couple is the centerpiece and you are the gorgeous frame. Think gilt, not *guilt*!

You need something figure flattering and age appropriate (this does not mean dowdy, it means sophisticated); maybe a below-the-knee dress in a subtle print or solid color that picks up the wedding colors. A rich, buttery, creamy satin seems perfect. Make sure whatever you choose is *clearly* a different color from the bride's dress. I don't encourage people to slavishly follow most style rules, but this one stands.

Can you believe you're one step closer to becoming a grandmother? (Don't worry, if you play your cards right, you'll look like you could be the bride's sister.) This is going to be one of the most amazing days of your life; try not to sweat the little things. Remember what this is all about: You're not losing a child, you're gaining a whole new family.

dream travel

CHIC TRANSIT

AND STYLISH ADVENTURING

On the Road Again

What to Wear When You're Traveling

Is that weird,
taking my Louis Vuitton bag camping?

JESSICA SIMPSON

Throwing a few essentials into a bag and heading off on a last-minute jaunt is one of life's sweetest pleasures. It doesn't matter where you're going: Escaping your daily routine, if only for a few precious days, recharges and replenishes you. I love the feeling of being on a plane just as it is about to land somewhere I've never been; I love the thrill of the unknown and the sense of wanderlust.

Through my many travels, I've learned to pack strategically, taking into account every possible detail of my forthcoming sojourn, however long or short. Next to a curious soul, the right clothes are the second-best traveling companion a woman could hope for.

The Luggage

An important element of travel is choosing the right luggage. You should have a sleek logo-free pull suitcase. Tumi, Samsonite, and Anya Hindmarch make marvelous luggage. Pack your toiletries in a pretty clutch that doubles as an evening bag. For quick getaways, carry a zippered oversize tote or weekender. LeSportsac has tons of options.

What to Wear to Get There

Every stylish traveler needs a go-to outfit for each major mode of transportation. I'm often perplexed by the women I see traipsing through the airport dressed to the nines, complete with stilettos. They look fabulous, but can you really pull your suitcase, carry your laptop, and find your passport while wearing six-inch heels? I'm infinitely more at ease in something more lounge-worthy, something you can be comfortable in even if you're stuck in an airport for eight hours.

The Plane, the Plane

Every day, it seems, enhanced airport security makes it a little more complicated to travel by air. You want to be the perfect combination of cozy and classy: cozy enough to endure the chilly AC in the airport and on the airplane and classy enough to look put together after an eight-hour flight. My in-flight ensemble is spill proof, wrinkle proof, and relaxed enough to sit in for long stretches of time. Think dark colors and soft, natural, knit fabrics that move with you and feel good against your skin. A pashmina keeps you warm and toasty for napping on the plane and works as a chic accessory once you've reached your destination. And ever since they've started asking us to remove our shoes, I've made sure to wear stockings or socks.

Do the Locomotion

There is nothing more romantic than traveling by train. If I had my choice, I would *always* travel by rail. The seats are roomy and you can gaze at the landscape gliding past your window while the rhythmic sound of the locomotive lulls you into a delightful nap. We've got to build more trains in the United States; the Europeans definitely know what they are doing when it comes to intra-continental travel.

What to wear? You can use the same go-to travel ensemble that you would fly in. But if you want to dress it up a bit, the roomier seats make wearing a suit or other tailored garments much easier.

The Long Car Ride

There's nothing like rolling along the highway with the window down while your favorite song plays on the car stereo—you are free as a bird and up for anything. There is something thrilling about the view whizzing by you. Even though you're in motion, time stands still. Unless you're packed in with small children or cranky adults, enjoy your time in what's essentially your own private VIP mode of transportation. Turn up the volume on the radio or listen to a great audiobook, and let time while away. When driving, your look should be as spill proof, wrinkle proof, and comfortable as anything you'd wear on a plane. Again, think dark colors and knits.

PANTS: Loose-fitting, beautifully draped pants, boyfriend jeans, or a pair of chic leggings.
TOP: Layers. Wear a tank or tee under a roomy button-down shirt or tunic with a light sweater. You'll feel at ease.
SHOES: Travel in flats: boots, loafers, sneakers. Choose a comfortable shoe that goes with other items in your suitcase.
ACCESSORIES: A scarf (always handy) and a watch (essential) are all you need.

> *Airplane travel is nature's way of making you look like your passport photo.*
>
> AL GORE

Dream Travel

These are the destinations that make us want to spontaneously quit our jobs and run to the nearest airport. Here are a few notes on what to wear when you get there.

R. Toledo

A Beach in Mustique

You're planning a week at one of my favorite places on the planet, the beach in Mustique. What do you pack? A bikini and not much else. This is the height of tropical paradise; beautiful beaches, gorgeous scenery—it's absolutely breathtaking. Bring your best bikinis, easy cotton tank dresses, one or two glamorous-island-night outfits, a sundress or two, and some sandals. You'll be able to tie sarongs expertly by the time you leave. Your best accessory is a bronze glow and the serenity radiating from within as you lounge on the sand. Be sure to stop at Basil's and order a Haroun or two. Pure heaven.

Paris in the Spring

Romance, rich history, even richer food, and nonstop fashion. And rain, so bring an umbrella. Parisian women are always flawlessly put together in that "I just rolled out of bed, put on some lipstick and whatever was handy, and look like I stepped out of a magazine" way. Bring one or two pairs of smart shoes and at least one casual pair. This is the birthplace of Coco Chanel and Christian Dior, both of whom reinvented the woman's suit. Honor them with impeccable style. Pack a tailored white shirt or two, a couple of chic knit tops, skinny jeans, a pencil skirt, a couple of jackets, and a little black dress. You just can't leave Paris empty-handed, so set aside a corner of your suitcase for new clothes. Trust me, you'll wish you had more space. All you need to round out your packing list are a trench coat and a bit of classic jewelry, such as a simple cuff and tasteful chandeliers. Then it's all baguettes and boulevards for you, my dear.

If you are lucky enough to have lived in Paris
as a young man, then wherever you go
for the rest of your life it stays with you,
for Paris is a moveable feast.

ERNEST HEMINGWAY

A Safari in Africa

Lions and elephants and my hair, oh my! There really are few things you'll experience that can top a week in Africa on a photo safari. (That's right—no guns, just photos.) Throw in a couple pairs of cargo pants (safari chic), a functional (but fabulous) sun hat, a couple of maxi dresses, and a pair of sandals for the evenings, and you're ready to meet even the most ferocious of God's creatures while looking picture perfect. Visit the local markets in Africa for textiles, beads, and baskets.

Iceland Spa

Reykjavík is a minimalist extravaganza. This may sound like an oxymoron, but you'll understand when you get there. Leave room in your suitcase for some of that gorgeous Icelandic wool. Pack sweaters and warm boots for days of shopping and visiting the phenomenal glaciers, and a swimsuit or two so you can lounge in one of the country's geothermal pools (an experience of pure healing, cleansing luxury). A visit to the Lauger Spa is mandatory. You'll leave flushed with a feeling of icy serenity. Be an Ice Queen, just this once.

A Weekend in the Hamptons

You scored an invite to P. Diddy's legendary White Party this summer, so it's off to the Hamptons, those surprisingly white-sanded beaches in Long Island, New York. Everyone, and I do mean everyone, from Sharon Stone to Sean Combs, will be giving you the up and down, so you've *got to* dress for this trip; the real key is to wear your finery as if it were an afterthought. Bring a few sophisticated disco looks, a stylish bikini for each day, and a lounge-happy Hamptons attitude.

Hiking in Patagonia

As soon as you book your trip, get a catalogue from the eponymous clothing company and outfit yourself with fabulous hiking gear. Then grab a copy of Bruce Chatwin's *In Patagonia* and get in touch with your inner pioneer.

This trip is exhausting, but afterward you'll be able to boast that you've been to one of the most beautiful places on earth. Do not forget your SPF.

Sailing on the Turkish Coast

The Aegean Sea, the Mediterranean, a luxury yacht, and twenty of your closest friends make for a perfect adventure on the high seas. You barely need to pack more than a large purse with a bikini and some sunscreen for this glorious cruise. Prepare for crystal blue water, sunning on the deck, and weighing anchor to hit the discos at night once you dock. Nibble on fresh grilled calamari and sip sweet tea. The most physical exertion you will have to deal with is cracking your pistachios open.

The Gardens (and Fashion) of Kyoto

Any true style connoisseur must make the fashion pilgrimage to Japan's Kyoto Costume Institute—home to one of the largest clothing collections in the world. If you can tear yourself away from this abundant inspiration, you might also want to see a few of Kyoto's sixteen hundred Buddhist temples (the Golden Temple is completely covered in gold!), or see the gardens located within each palace and villa. Pack plenty of Yohji Yamamoto and Limi Feu.

The Taj Mahal

What does a girl bring on a visit to one of the Eight Wonders of the World? Plenty of room in her suitcase for breathtaking Indian textiles; an array of sundresses, sandals, and shawls; and comfy walking shoes. Of course, bring a camera and why not a journal? Dare to have your own *Eat, Pray, Love* adventure and look smashing the whole time. Om Shanti chic doesn't require much effort.

A Helicopter Ride over the Grand Canyon

Nothing says pure decadence like a helicopter flight over the Grand Canyon—yet the spectacular view of nature is deeply humbling. Bring sunglasses and Dramamine, and a really good camera.

A Gondola Ride through the Canals of Venice

The food is heavenly, of course, so make sure you pack clothing with a variety of waistlines. You're going to need extra carb room. But if you can pack only one special item for your trip to Venice, make it a fantastic pair of shoes. The Italians take their footwear *very* seriously, and you know what they say: *when in Rome*. The icon is Sophia Loren, the mood is a Fellini film, and the designer is Dolce & Gabbana.

Hair: A Glossary

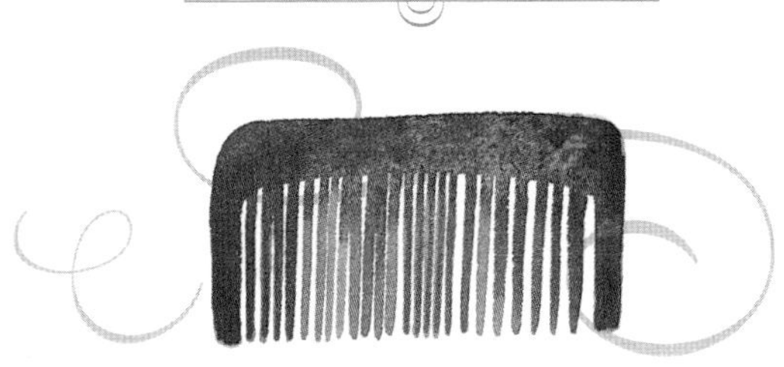

LONG AND LOOSE: This style says you're cool and at ease. It's a casual, low-maintenance look.

SHORT AND SASSY: Excellent bone structure is a prerequisite for a super-short do. Short hair is sporty, daring, and very chic.

BLUNT BOB: Louise Brooks did it best. This can be a severe look. It's a strong, assertive style that highlights a swanlike neck beautifully.

BRAID: Braids are fun and a great way to disguise overstressed hair. Incorporating a mini French braid into a longer style is a fresh, playful approach.

PONYTAIL: A low, sleek ponytail is ultra chic and polished. A messy ponytail swept slightly to the side is sexy and modern.

CHIGNON: Elegant and sophisticated. Perfect for a formal event or an all-business look.

MESSY BUN: Up high, at the nape, or off to the side. A tousled bun is the modern updo.

BANGS: Long bangs, swept to the side or straight to your eyes, are an edgy, sexy way to update your do.

Afterword

Adventure is not outside man; it is within.

GEORGE ELIOT

I adore everything about the theatrics of dressing, the art of design, and the creativity of style. Fashion is always evolving—borrowing from the past but predicting the future. This constant motion keeps fashion alive and exciting. It also keeps many women in a state of confusion about what to wear, how to wear it, and when. Now that you've perused my collection of looks for many of life's events, you're on your way to being the best-dressed woman at any function. And, at the very least, you'll be less stressed when deciding what to wear.

In the twenty-first century, the fashion rules will continue to get broader and broader. I love the new freedom women have with style. But having so many options can get overwhelming. If you take any ideas from my *Look Book* (and I certainly hope you do), remember that these are meant only as suggestions upon which you can build your own individual style. Think of them as a gentle boost to give you the confidence to put together fabulous ensembles that reflect you, that communicate your personal message at any occasion.

Remind yourself that glamour is what you make of it—a great pair of jeans and a tee can be glamorous if you spice them up with great shoes and a few key accessories. Never get too caught up with logos or brand names. Runway looks are fabulous reference points to stimulate your imagination and develop your style vision, but never think you must spend a fortune in order to achieve a dazzling look. Understand what flatters you, and wear it unapologetically.

When in doubt, remember these four mantras. They cost nothing. And offer everything.

Be comfortable.
Be confident.
Proper fit is vital.
Wear it like you mean it.

The way the world reacts to *how* you wear an ensemble can open doors, create opportunities, and help make life a dazzling adventure. Never let yourself down, or let the world down, by not living up to your style standards. Trust me on this.

—*Nina*

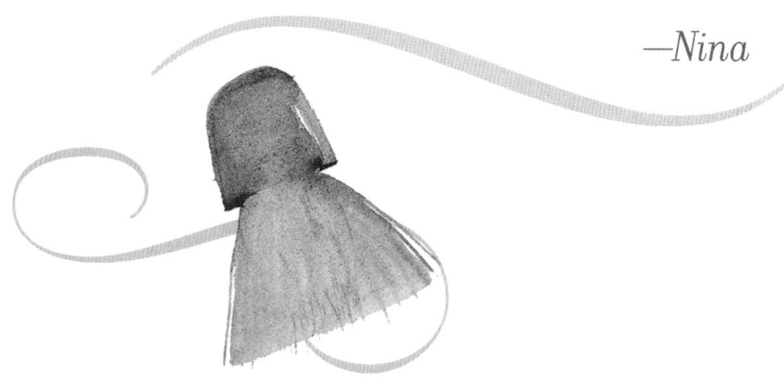

Acknowledgments

Thanks to David and Lucas, for continuing to inspire me, and for bringing joy and fulfillment to everything you touch.

Ruben Toledo is, and will always be, one of the world's most talented visual masters. As it has been in the past, and will always be, collaborating with him brings me sheer joy.

Rene Alegria continues to amaze me. As do Christina Saratsis and Vanessa Binder. This book would not be possible without you each doing what you do so very, very well.

Thanks to all the people at Voice, the imprint of Hyperion Books by and for women, for making this book possible. Each and every one of you is truly the best at what you do, especially Ellen Archer, Barbara Jones, Claire McKean, Shubhani Sarkar, Betsy Wilson, and Rachel Durfee.

To Heidi, Tim, Michael, Joanna Coles, and all the other talented people at *Marie Claire*, Lifetime, and *Project Runway*: All of you make every day an exciting one. I cannot begin to express how grateful I am for that.

p. 201
p. 131
p. 183
p. 257
p. 215
p. 267
p. 303
p. 246
p. 73
p. 270
p. 293